Alsace Travel Guide 2023-2024

The Essential Guide to Exploring France's Finest Wine Region

COLMAR
JAMES BOUTIQUE HOTEL

Mayra Harvey

TABLE OF CONTENTS

INTRODUCTION 9

    HISTORY 11

    WHY VISIT ALSACE 13

CHAPTER 1 17

    GETTING TO ALSACE 17

- TRANSPORTATION OPTIONS 17
- LOCAL TRANSPORTATION WITHIN ALSACE 20

CHAPTER 2 23

    BEST TIME TO VISIT ALSACE 23

- CLIMATE AND WEATHER PATTERN 23
- PEAK TOURIST SEASONS 26
- OFF-SEASON BENEFITS 29

CHAPTER 3 33

    EXPLORING ALSACES'S CITIES AND TOWNS 33

- STRASBOURG 33
- COLMAR 37
- MULHOUSE 41
- RIQUEWIHR 44

- EGUISHEIM.. 47

- OTHER CHARMING VILLAGES 50

CHAPTER 4 53

MUST-VISIT ATTRACTIONS IN ALSACE 53

- ALSACE WINE ROUTE 53

- STRASBOURG CATHEDRAL....................................... 56

- HAUT-KOENIGSBOURG CASTLE 59

- PETITE FRANCE 62

- UNTERLINDEN MUSEUM... 66

- EUROPA-PARK... 69

CHAPTER 5 73

OUTDOOR ACTIVITIES IN ALSACE 73

- HIKING AND NATURE TRAILS 73

Hiking Essentials 73

Top Hiking and Nature Trails in Alsace 74

- CYCLING ROUTES 76

- WATER SPORTS AND RIVER CRUISES..................... 79

- SKIING AND WATER SPORTS 82

Skiing in Alsace 82

CHAPTER 6 87

ALSACE'S CULINARY DELIGHTS 87

- TRADITIONAL ALSATIAN CUISINE.......................... 87

- FAMOUS ALSATIAN DISHES................................. 88

- LOCAL WINES AND VINEYARD 90

- FOOD FESTIVALS AND MARKETS.......................... 94

Food Festivals and Markets 94

CHAPTER 7 97

ACCOMMODATION OPTIONS IN ALSACE 97

- LUXURY HOTELS AND RESORTS 97

- CHARMING BED AND BREAKFASTS...................... 101

- BUDGET-FRIENDLY ACCOMMODATIONS............ 104

- UNIQUE STAYS: CASTLE AND VINEYARD
LODGINGS 108

CHAPTER 8 111

PLANNING YOUR ALSACE ITINERARY...................... 111

- RECOMMENDED DURATION OF STAY 111

- TIPS FOR EFFICIENT SIGHTSEEING........................ 113

CHAPTER 9 117

PRACTICAL INFORMATION AND TRAVEL TIPS.......... 117

CURRENCY... 117

- LANGUAGE ABD COMMUNICATION 120

- SAFETY AND EMERGENCY CONTACTS................. 124

- LOCAL CUSTOMS AND ETIQUETTE....................... 127

- PACKING ESSENTIALS 130

- ANNUAL FESTIVALS AND CELEBRATIONS.......... 133

CONCLUSION... 137

INTRODUCTION

Welcome to a region where history blends effortlessly into the fabric of the present, cobblestone streets whisper stories of ages past, and cultural fusion provides an experience unlike any other. Step into Alsace, an idyllic area tucked in the heart of Europe, where vineyards extend as far as the eye can see, ancient villages ooze a timeless beauty, and a rich tapestry of traditions awaits your discovery.

Prepare to go on a trip that goes beyond simply sightseeing as you read through our Alsace travel guide for 2023-2024. History and modernity live together in this area, enabling you to meander through picturesque towns where half-timbered buildings remain as living testaments to the country's historic past. Travel the fabled Alsace Wine Route, a winding journey over rolling hills that promises not only superb wines but also immersion in a country where viticulture is a way of life.

Our trip will reveal the architectural treasures of Strasbourg, the cosmopolitan capital of the area, where the landmark Strasbourg Cathedral soars for the sky and the combination of French and German influences is felt on every street corner.

Explore Alsace's gastronomic wonders, where meaty delicacies like choucroute garnie and flammekueche tempt the taste, and Michelin-starred restaurants elevate eating to an art form.

But Alsace is more than just a sensory experience; it's a domain of discovery for the inquisitive spirit. Discover the Maginot Line's echoes of World War II history, gaze in amazement at the Haut-Koenigsbourg Castle, which overlooks the countryside, and interact with warm-hearted inhabitants who are the living embodiment of Alsace's hospitality.

Whether you're a history buff, a wine connoisseur, a gourmet adventurer, or a seeker of one-of-a-kind experiences, Alsace welcomes you with open arms. Our travel guide is your key to discovering the region's hidden gems, exciting festivals, and compelling tales. So, let the pages of this book serve as your portal to an amazing trip in Alsace, where time-honored traditions and modern wonders mingle to create a tapestry of wonder that will linger with you long after your tour is over.

HISTORY

1. **Ancient Origins:** Alsace's history may be traced back to ancient times when it was inhabited by Celtic tribes. The region's strategic position led to its absorption into the Roman Empire, contributing to its cultural and economic growth. Roman settlements and highways created during this time still left their imprint on the environment.

2. **Medieval Era:** The Middle Ages saw the advent of feudalism in Alsace, with various local lords asserting power over the province. A crucial occasion was the founding of the Holy Roman Empire, which placed Alsace under its dominion. The influence of the Catholic Church rose, evidenced in the building of beautiful churches, such as Strasbourg Cathedral.

3. **Hostilities and Shifts:** Alsace's strategic importance sometimes made it a battlefield during hostilities. The Hundred Years' War and the Thirty Years' War had enormous impacts on the area, resulting in territory swaps between France and the Holy Roman Empire. The Peace of Westphalia in 1648 represented a turning point, bringing portions of Alsace under French authority while other sections remained with the Empire.

4. **Cultural Diversity:** Throughout its history, Alsace has been a melting pot of cultures and languages. Its location at the intersection of Germanic and Romance civilizations has formed its distinctive

personality. The Alsatian vernacular, integrating German and French components, is a witness to this cultural fusion.

5. **Annexation by France:** The late 17th century saw the bulk of Alsace fall under French authority during the Franco-Dutch War. Under Louis XIV, the area was subject to centralization and assimilation programs, yet local customs and identities were maintained.

6. **Modernization and Industrialization:** The 19th century brought considerable changes to Alsace. Industrialization turned communities like Mulhouse into bustling textile hubs. However, the Franco-Prussian War of 1870-71 led to Alsace's annexation by the newly united Germany, resulting in modifications in language, culture, and governance.

7. **World Wars and Reconciliation:** The 20th century offered unprecedented problems. Alsace witnessed the horrors of two World Wars, with its position moving between France and Germany. The region's residents faced tough decisions as they negotiated shifting allegiances.

8. **Contemporary Alsace:** Following World War II, Alsace was reintegrated into France. The region's distinctive character and history earned recognized, and attempts were undertaken to conserve its cultural legacy. Today, Alsace flourishes as a

combination of history and modernity, encouraging tourists to discover its gorgeous towns, wineries, and cultural treasures.

WHY VISIT ALSACE

1. Historical Significance and Architectural Marvels:

Alsace's history is evident as you meander through its cobblestone alleyways, each corner echoing stories of medieval ages, conflicts, and diplomacy. The region's strategic position along the Rhine River has made it a battlefield for ages, leaving behind a path of castles, fortresses, and medieval cities. The Alsace Wine Route, studded with lovely half-timbered buildings, is a superb illustration of the region's architectural history. The magnificent Strasbourg Cathedral, a marvel of Gothic architecture, remains a tribute to the creative brilliance of its creators.

2. Unique Cultural Fusion:

The region's identity is a magnificent mix of French and German traditions. Centuries of shared history have resulted in a fascinating combination of languages, rituals, and festivals. The Alsace dialect, a combination of French and German, is still spoken by certain locals, showing the linguistic legacy of the region. Local festivities like the Strasbourg Christmas Market and the Colmar Wine Fair capture this unique blend, relying on both traditions to produce spectacular celebrations.

3. Enchanting Villages:

Alsace is peppered with an assortment of gorgeous villages that appear right out of a fairy tale. Colmar, commonly referred to as the "Little Venice" of Alsace, enchants tourists with its canals, colorful buildings, and flower-filled alleys. Riquewihr, with its well-preserved medieval beauty, takes you back in time as you meander through its small streets. Eguisheim, a round hamlet, is recognized for its concentric construction and wonderful ambiance.

4. World-Class Wine and Vineyards:

The undulating hills of Alsace are decorated with precisely managed vineyards that produce some of the best wines in the world. The area is recognized for its white wines, notably Riesling, Gewürztraminer, and Pinot Gris. Wine connoisseurs may go on a tour along the Alsace Wine Route, visiting family-owned wineries, tasting cellars, and learning about the delicate art of winemaking.

5. Culinary Delights:

Alsace is a gourmet wonderland that tantalizes the taste buds with its rich culinary history. Traditional foods like Choucroute Garnie (sauerkraut with sausages and meats), Flammekueche (thin crust pizza-like dish), and Baeckeoffe (slow-cooked casserole) are a tribute to the region's robust cuisine. The food is generally distinguished by the use of locally obtained ingredients, resulting in tastes that are both soothing and excellent.

6. **Natural Beauty:**

The Alsace area provides stunning scenery that ranges from the Vosges Mountains to the tranquil Rhine River. Nature enthusiasts may explore the Parc Naturel Régional des Ballons des Vosges, a protected region featuring hiking paths, alpine meadows, and breathtaking vistas. The scenic Route des Crêtes travels through the Vosges, giving tourists to magnificent panoramas of the surrounding countryside.

7. **Warm Hospitality:**

Alsace is noted for its hospitable and friendly residents who are ready to share their culture and customs. Whether you're touring a little town or eating at a local restaurant, you'll frequently find that the people of Alsace are more than happy to participate in discussions and share insights into their way of life.

ALSACE TRAVEL GUIDE 2023-2024

CHAPTER 1

GETTING TO ALSACE

• TRANSPORTATION OPTIONS

1. **Public Transportation:**

1.1 *Trains:* France boasts a vast and efficient rail network, and Alsace is no exception. The area is well-connected to large cities like Paris and Lyon with high-speed trains (TGV). Strasbourg acts as a center for rail travel in Alsace, giving links to many places within the area and beyond. The TER (Transport Express Régional) trains allow quick access to smaller towns and villages, making it simple to visit the heart of Alsace.

1.2 *Trams and Buses:* Strasbourg features an outstanding tram system that makes moving around the city a snap. The city's well-designed tram network links significant areas of interest, including the European institutions and the old city center. Buses supplement the tram system and are especially beneficial for accessing regions not directly serviced by trams.

2. **Car Rentals:**

2.1 *Renting a vehicle:* Renting a vehicle in Alsace allows the opportunity to explore at your speed and visit rural regions that may not be readily available by public transit. Rental firms may be located at major airports, railway stations, and city centers. Keep in mind that driving in the city centers of cities like Strasbourg and Colmar might be problematic owing to tight streets and restricted parking.

2.2 *Road Conditions:* Roads in Alsace are typically well-maintained, making driving a pleasant alternative. Be prepared for tolls on certain motorways (autoroutes), and educate yourself about local traffic laws and regulations.

3. **Biking:**

3.1 *Bike Rentals:* Alsace is a cyclist-friendly area, with designated bike trails that pass through stunning landscapes. Many cities and towns have bike rental services, enabling you to visit picturesque villages and vineyards at a leisurely pace.

3.2 *Bike Routes:* The Alsace Wine Path (Route des Vins) is a popular bike path that takes you through picturesque vineyards, ancient towns, and gorgeous scenery. This route gives a unique chance to appreciate the region's culture, history, and wines while riding.

4. **Walking:**

4.1 *Exploring on Foot:* Alsace's towns and cities are typically best visited on foot owing to their small size and lovely architecture. Strasbourg's Grand Île, a UNESCO World Heritage site, is a pedestrian-friendly region that encompasses the city's historical and architectural splendor.

4.2 *Guided Tours:* Joining walking tours in towns like Strasbourg and Colmar enables you to explore further their history, culture, and tales. Knowledgeable guides give insights into local culture, architecture, and hidden jewels.

5. River Transportation:

5.1 *Boat trips:* The Rhine River runs along Alsace's eastern border, allowing chances for boat trips. These trips give a distinct view of the region's landscapes and towns, including Strasbourg.

5.2 *European Waterways:* The canals and waterways that connect Alsace may be visited by river cruises. These cruises sometimes include excursions to lovely towns and cultural places along the way.

• LOCAL TRANSPORTATION WITHIN ALSACE

1. **Trains:** Efficient and Scenic Journeys

The railroad network in Alsace is broad and efficient, making it a popular alternative for both inhabitants and visitors. The main cities of Alsace, such as Strasbourg, Colmar, and Mulhouse, are well-connected by regular and pleasant rail services. The high-speed TGV (Train à Grande Vitesse) links Alsace to major French cities including Paris, Lyon, and Marseille.

2. **Trams:** Convenient Intra-city Travel

Trams are a prominent means of transit inside several Alsace cities, notably in Strasbourg. Strasbourg features an extensive tram network that includes the city's major attractions and districts. The trams are contemporary and clean, and provide a handy method to navigate the city.

3. **Buses**: Connecting Smaller Towns

Buses are a key element of the local transportation network, linking smaller towns and villages that may not have direct rail or tram connections. The bus network is well-maintained, enabling access to more isolated places and allowing you to visit off-the-beaten-path attractions.

4. **Biking:** Embrace Eco-Friendly Exploration

Alsace is famed for its stunning scenery, and riding is a fantastic opportunity to immerse oneself in its splendor. Many municipalities provide bike rental services, and well-marked bike lanes weave through vineyards, along canals, and through picturesque villages. It's a sustainable and entertaining way to explore the countryside at your leisure.

5. **Car Rentals:** Flexibility and Freedom

Renting a vehicle allows the opportunity to explore Alsace on your terms. This is particularly beneficial if you wish to visit rural villages or explore the Alsace Wine Route at your leisure. Roads are well-maintained, and traveling through the region's stunning surroundings may be a pleasant experience.

6. **Taxis and Ridesharing**: On-Demand Convenience

Taxis and ridesharing services are accessible in major cities and towns, giving handy transportation choices, especially for short distances or when public transit may not be easily available. Keep in mind that these solutions might be more costly compared to public transit.

7. **River Transportation:** Discover Alsace from the Water

The Rhine River runs along the eastern border of Alsace, and several cities offer river cruises or boat trips. These unique excursions enable you to explore Alsace's countryside from a fresh perspective while enjoying a leisurely tour.

8. **Travel Passes and Cards:** Economical Choices

Consider obtaining travel passes or cards if you expect to utilize public transit often. The Alsace Pass, for example, enables unlimited travel on trains, trams, and buses throughout the area. It might be a cost-effective choice for exploring numerous areas.

CHAPTER 2

BEST TIME TO VISIT ALSACE

• CLIMATE AND WEATHER PATTERN

Understanding Alsace's Climate: Alsace has a moderate climate affected by its position between the Vosges Mountains and the Rhine River. The area enjoys four unique seasons, each adding to the richness of experiences for guests.

Spring (March-May):

Temperature Range: 7°C to 17°C (45°F to 63°F)

Characteristic Weather: Spring is a lovely season to visit Alsace, with flowers flowering, and the landscape becoming lush and green. The weather starts to climb, and outside activities become more delightful.

Summer (June - August):

Temperature Range: 15°C to 27°C (59°F to 81°F)

Characteristic Weather: Summers in Alsace are warm and pleasant, making it excellent for visiting the region's outdoor attractions. The vineyards are at their most colorful, and events abound.

Autumn (September - November):

Temperature Range: 7°C to 17°C (45°F to 63°F)

Characteristic Weather: The autumn leaves turn the environment into a symphony of warm hues. The weather stays pleasant, and the grape harvest season brings a joyous spirit to the vineyards.

Winter (December - February):

Temperature Range: -1°C to 6°C (30°F to 43°F)

Characteristic Weather: Winter in Alsace is frigid yet lovely. The region's Christmas markets are a big attraction, presenting a lovely environment with dazzling lights and traditional goods. Snowfall is likely, accentuating the gorgeous surroundings.

Planning for the Seasons:

Spring and summer:

Pack lightweight clothes, sunscreen, and comfortable walking shoes.

Explore the Alsatian Wine Route, explore Strasbourg's historic area, and indulge in outdoor sports like cycling and hiking.

Autumn:

Bring layers to adjust to shifting temperatures.

Join in the grape harvest celebrations and enjoy the region's famous wines.

Wander around the lovely alleys of Colmar and Riquewihr as they exhibit their October splendor.

Winter:

Bundle up with warm clothes, gloves, and a comfortable scarf.

Immerse yourself in the magic of Christmas markets, such as Strasbourg's Christkindelsmärik.

Visit the Haut-Koenigsbourg Castle for spectacular winter vistas.

Local Tips for Weather Preparedness:

Check Weather predictions: Stay informed with local weather predictions to organize your daily activities appropriately.

Layering: Given the temperature changes during the day, layering your apparel promotes comfort throughout your adventures.

Umbrella: Carry a tiny umbrella in case of unexpected rain showers.

Hydration and Sun Protection: Regardless of the season, keeping hydrated and protecting oneself from the sun's rays is vital.

• PEAK TOURIST SEASONS

1. Alsace

Alsace features a unique combination of French and German influences owing to its volatile history of transferring hands between the two nations. This is visible in its architecture, food, and local customs. The area is distinguished by beautiful medieval villages, extensive vineyards, and the breathtaking background of the Vosges Mountains.

2. Spring (March through May)

Spring is a beautiful time to visit Alsace as the area erupts into vivid hues with blossoming flowers and verdant scenery. The weather begins to warm up, making it great for visiting outdoor sites. The main tourist season starts around April, notably around Easter vacations.

3. Summer (June through August)

Summer is the prime season for tourism in Alsace, luring visitors with its pleasant weather and countless activities. The area comes alive with festivals, outdoor markets, and numerous cultural events. It's suggested to reserve lodgings and activities in advance owing to the high demand.

Highlights:

Alsace Wine Festivals: Experience the famed wine festivals in places like Riquewihr and Eguisheim.

Hiking and Biking: Explore the Vosges Mountains with a selection of outdoor sports.

Traditional Cuisine: Indulge in Alsatian delicacies like tarte flambée and choucroute garnie.

4. Fall (September through November)

Fall, often known as the wine harvest season, is a compelling time to visit Alsace. The vineyards convert into a palette of golden and scarlet colors, creating a magnificent ambiance. The weather stays warm, and the crowds start to thin out, giving it an excellent time for a leisurely tour.

Highlights:

Wine Harvest Celebrations: Participate in grape harvesting activities and wine-related celebrations.

Scenic Drives: Drive along the wine trails and savor the gorgeous autumn colors.

Museums & Galleries: Discover Alsace's rich history and cultural legacy at local museums.

5. Winter (December through February)

Winter in Alsace brings a distinct type of appeal with its festive markets and warm environment. While it's considered the off-peak season, the region's Christmas markets are famed and draw people from all around. The chilly temperature adds to the snug ambiance, suitable for enjoying indoor attractions.

Highlights:

Christmas Markets: Strasbourg's Christkindelsmärik is one of the oldest and most known Christmas markets in Europe.

Alsace Cuisine: Warm up with substantial foods like baeckeoffe and mulled wine.

Château Visits: Tour historic castles amid a background of snow-covered landscapes.

- ## OFF-SEASON BENEFITS

1. Intimate Cultural Experiences:

One of the major benefits of visiting Alsace during the off-season is the ability to immerse yourself in the region's rich culture without the crowds. Museums, historical buildings, and local attractions are frequently less crowded, providing for a more personalized encounter.

You may take your time touring prominent places such as Strasbourg's majestic Gothic cathedral, the Strasbourg Historical Museum, or the Haut-Koenigsbourg Castle with fewer people, fostering a stronger connection with the local culture and heritage.

2. Culinary Delights:

Alsace is recognized for its superb culinary scene, merging French and German elements to produce a distinct gourmet experience. During the off-season, local restaurants and cafés give a more real flavor of Alsace cuisine, as you connect with locals and sample traditional delicacies like choucroute garnie (sauerkraut with sausages), tarte flambée (Alsatian pizza), and a range of robust stews.

Additionally, visiting vineyards during the off-season allows an opportunity to engage in meaningful talks with winemakers and enjoy wine tastings in a more relaxed situation.

3. Festivals & Events:

While Alsace organizes various colorful festivals and events throughout the year, the off-season lends its particular appeal to these festivities. The Christmas markets in places like Strasbourg and Colmar are world-famous, converting the area into a winter paradise. The off-season also gives the possibility to attend local activities that could be overlooked during the busy season. From traditional Alsatian folk festivals to art exhibits and classical music concerts, you'll have the chance to participate in the local culture on a deeper level.

4. Tranquil Landscapes:

The off-season enables you to admire the natural beauty of Alsace in a serene setting. While the vineyards may not be rich with grapes, the picturesque grandeur of the undulating hills and lovely communities is ever-present. Imagine enjoying strolls down cobblestone lanes dotted with half-timbered buildings, capturing the charm of the country without the congestion and bustle of peak tourist crowds.

5. Budget-Friendly Travel:

Traveling during the off-season frequently means reduced pricing for lodgings, airlines, and tourist sites. This budget-friendly element of off-season travel may make your vacation to Alsace more cheap and accessible, enabling you to focus your resources on unique experiences and gastronomic pleasures that the area has to offer.

6. **Personalized Hospitality**:

With fewer visitors around, you're likely to enjoy more customized and attentive treatment from locals in hotels, restaurants, and stores. This allows you to engage more with the inhabitants and acquire insight into their everyday lives and customs. The warmth and kindness of the Alsatian people show even more when the area is less populated.

ALSACE TRAVEL GUIDE 2023-2024

CHAPTER 3

EXPLORING ALSACES'S CITIES AND TOWNS

• STRASBOURG

1. **Getting There**

Strasbourg is well-connected by plane, rail, and road. The Strasbourg International Airport serves flights from major European cities. Alternatively, you may take a high-speed rail (TGV) from Paris, Frankfurt, or other neighboring cities. If you prefer vehicle travel, the city is accessible through the A4 and A35 roads.

2. **Accommodation**

Strasbourg provides a broad selection of hotel alternatives to suit all budgets. From elegant hotels along the riverbank to quaint bed & breakfasts in the old town, you'll find something that meets your interests. Consider staying in the historic center to be near most attractions.

3. **Sightseeing and Activities**

A. *Strasbourg Cathedral (Cathédrale Notre-Dame)*

This marvel of Gothic architecture serves as a symbol of the city. Climb the 332 steps to the summit for a stunning panoramic view of Strasbourg and the surrounding region.

B. *La Petite France*

This attractive area is famed for its half-timbered buildings, charming canals, and flower-lined walkways. It's a fantastic area for strolls and shooting postcard-worthy photographs.

C. *Palais Rohan*

Examine the three museums—the Museum of Fine Arts, the Archaeological Museum, and the Museum of Decorative Arts—that are housed in the medieval palace. The magnificent rooms and rich collections are a delight for art and history buffs.

D. *Boat Tour on the Ill River*

Embark on a leisurely boat cruise to discover Strasbourg from a fresh viewpoint. Glide beneath lovely bridges and past historical sites while learning about the city's history.

E. *European Parliament*

Strasbourg is a seat of European institutions, notably the European Parliament. Check the session calendar and join discussions or guided tours to learn about the European Union's activities.

4. Cuisine

Alsace is recognized for its rich and savory food. Don't miss out on sampling these local delicacies:

A. *Choucroute Garnie*

A dish of fermented cabbage served with different sausages, potatoes, and occasionally meat. It's a distinctive Alsatian meal that mixes German and French flavors.

B. *Tarte Flambée (Flammkuchen)*

A thin-crust pizza-like meal topped with crème fraîche, onions, and bacon. It's ideal for sharing and works nicely with local wines.

C. *Munster Cheese Sample*

This strong-smelling cheese that's a regional specialty. It's commonly eaten on its own or in meals like tarts and quiches.

5. Shopping

Explore the local markets and stores to locate unique souvenirs and presents. Rue des Hallebardes and Rue du Maroquin are fantastic lanes for shopping, providing everything from apparel to handicrafts.

6. Transportation

Getting about Strasbourg is straightforward with an extensive tram network and well-connected bus lines. Consider obtaining a Strasbourg Pass for unlimited public transit and reduced access to attractions.

7. Best Time to Visit

The ideal time to visit Strasbourg is during the spring (April to June) and autumn (September to October) when the weather is nice, and the city is less congested. The Christmas market in December is also a fantastic experience.

8. Local Etiquette

Remember to greet locals with a courteous "Bonjour" and thank them with "Merci." It's also typical to wait for the host to give a toast before taking a drink during meals.

9. Safety Tips

Strasbourg is typically secure, but like any city, be careful with your goods in busy places and keep aware of your surroundings, particularly at night.

• COLMAR

1. Getting There and Around

By Air: The closest major airport is EuroAirport Basel-Mulhouse-Freiburg, which is roughly 55 kilometers distant. From there, you may take a train or hire a vehicle to reach Colmar.

By rail: Colmar is well-connected by rail, with frequent connections from major cities including Strasbourg, Paris, and Basel. The railway station is conveniently positioned within walking distance of the town center.

By Car: If you prefer driving, Colmar may be readily accessed through the A35 highway. Parking is accessible, although it's encouraged to utilize public transit or walk throughout the town owing to its tiny size.

2. Accommodation Options

Colmar provides a selection of lodging alternatives to meet any traveler's interests and budget. From charming guesthouses and boutique hotels in the historic neighborhood to contemporary motels near the railway station, you'll find a pleasant place to stay.

3. Exploring the Old Town

The heart of Colmar is its well-preserved ancient town, where every nook appears to be taken from a fairytale. Highlights include:

La Petite Venise: A area known for its canals, flower-filled bridges, and colorful buildings.

Maison des Têtes: An beautiful Renaissance structure filled with statues of heads, affording a look into the town's past architecture.

St. Martin's Church: A Gothic masterpiece including gorgeous stained glass windows and an amazing organ.

4. **Museums and Cultural Attractions**

Colmar features a variety of museums that dive into its rich history and culture:

Unterlinden Museum: Housed in a former convent, this museum shows a remarkable collection of art, including the renowned Isenheim Altarpiece.

Bartholdi Museum: Learn about the life and work of Frédéric Auguste Bartholdi, the sculptor of the Statue of Liberty.

5. **Culinary Delights**

Alsace is famed for its wonderful gastronomy, and Colmar is no exception:

Tarte Flambée: A thin, crispy pizza-like dish topped with cream, onions, and bacon.

Choucroute: A robust meal incorporating sauerkraut, sausages, and other meats.

Alsace Wine: Explore local vineyards and luxuriate in Alsatian wines like Riesling and Gewürztraminer.

6. Festivals and Events

Experience the colorful ambiance of Colmar by visiting its different festivals and events:

Christmas Markets: Colmar's seasonal markets are a sight to see, converting the town into a winter paradise.

Fête de la Musique: A music event marking the summer solstice with concerts across the town.

7. Day Trips

Consider traveling outside Colmar to explore the neighboring area:

Riquewihr: A adjacent medieval town notable for its well-preserved architecture and vineyards.

Eguisheim: Another picturesque town with a circular plan and colorful dwellings.

8. **Practical Tips**

Language: French and Alsatian German are the predominant languages spoken. Basic French phrases would be beneficial.

Currency: The currency utilized is the Euro (EUR).

Climate: Colmar has a continental climate, with warm summers and chilly winters. Pack properly dependent on the season of your vacation.

9. **Respect Local Customs**

While in Colmar, observe local customs and traditions. It's usual to greet individuals with a courteous "Bonjour" and "Au revoir."

- ## MULHOUSE

1. Getting There

Mulhouse is readily accessible by numerous kinds of transportation:

By Air: The EuroAirport Basel-Mulhouse-Freiburg serves the area, providing international and local flights.

By railway: The Mulhouse-Ville railway station links the city to major French and European cities by high-speed trains.

By automobile: Mulhouse is well-connected by roads, making it handy for people going by automobile.

2. Accommodation

Mulhouse has a selection of lodging alternatives to meet various budgets and preferences:

Luxury Hotels: Experience top-notch hospitality at luxury hotels like Hotel du Parc and Hotel Bristol.

Mid-Range Hotels: Options like Hotel Novotel and Hotel Kyriad provide comfort without breaking the budget.

Boutique Stays: Explore unique local stays in lovely boutique hotels and guesthouses.

3. Must-Visit Attractions

Cité de l'Automobile: Discover one of the world's biggest vehicle museums, featuring a spectacular collection of historic and unusual cars.

Cité du Train: Explore the French National Railway Museum, including an astonishing collection of old trains and engines.

Mulhouse Zoo: Spend a day at the Parc Zoologique et Botanique de Mulhouse, home to a vast assortment of animals and gorgeous botanical gardens.

Temple Saint-Étienne: Admire the spectacular architecture of this Protestant church, a historic monument in the city center.

4. Cultural Experiences Museums Galore

Immerse yourself in art, history, and science at museums including the Musée des Beaux-Arts, Musée Historique de Mulhouse, and Ecomusée d'Alsace.

Theatre & Music: Check out the schedule at La Filature, a famous performing arts center, for theater, music, and dance acts.

Alsace Cuisine: Indulge in Alsatian delicacies like tarte flambée, choucroute garnie, and pretzels at local restaurants and traditional winstubs.

5. Outdoor Adventures in the Vosges Mountains

Embark on hiking paths in the Vosges Mountains, affording panoramic views of the Alsace area.

Biking lanes: Explore the city and its surroundings by bike along well-marked riding lanes.

6. Shopping and Souvenirs Markets

Shop for local vegetables, crafts, and antiques in the Marché du Canal Couvert and the Christmas markets throughout the holiday season.

Textile stores: Mulhouse has a great history in textiles; explore stores like the Cité de l'Habitat for fabrics and home furnishings.

7. Nearby Day Trips

Colmar: Explore the lovely town of Colmar, noted for its well-preserved medieval buildings and attractive waterways.

Strasbourg: Visit the capital of Alsace, noted for its majestic cathedral, medieval old town, and European institutions.

8. Travel Tips Language

While French is the official language, many inhabitants also know English and German owing to the region's history.

Currency: The currency utilized is the Euro (EUR).

Local Etiquette: It's traditional to greet shops and service employees with a courteous "Bonjour" before initiating a discussion.

Transport Passes: Consider getting the Alsace Pass for unrestricted access to public transit and savings on attractions.

- ## RIQUEWIHR

1. Getting There:

Riquewihr is conveniently accessible by many kinds of transportation. The closest major airport is Strasbourg Airport, around an hour's drive away. Alternatively, you may take a train to Colmar, which is approximately 20 minutes from Riquewihr, and then utilize local transit or a cab to reach the hamlet.

2. Housing:

Riquewihr provides a selection of housing alternatives to suit varied budgets and interests. From quaint boutique hotels to quiet guesthouses, you'll find lots of options that represent the village's typical Alsatian architecture and friendliness.

3. Exploring the Village:

3.1 *Historic Old Town:* Stroll through the cobblestone lanes of Riquewihr's ancient old town, surrounded by well-preserved medieval houses embellished with colorful half-timbered facades.

The village's layout has remained mostly intact throughout the ages, providing a sensation of going back in time.

3.2 *Musée de la Communication en Alsace:* Visit this fascinating museum to learn about the history of communication and printing in the Alsace area. The museum features diverse instruments, printing machines, and exhibitions that reflect the growth of communication systems.

4. Wine Tasting:

4.1 *Alsace Wines*: Riquewihr is located in the heart of Alsace's wine district. Take advantage of the various wine cellars and tasting rooms that provide an opportunity to experience the region's famous white wines, such as Riesling, Gewürztraminer, and Pinot Gris. Learn about the wine-making process and the terroir that gives these wines their special flavor.

5. Culinary Delights:

5.1 *Alsatian Cuisine:* Indulge in the delights of Alsatian cuisine in the village's lovely restaurants and cafés. Try typical foods like tarte flambée (a thin, delicious flatbread), choucroute garnie (sauerkraut with sausages and other meats), and baeckeoffe (a substantial meat and vegetable stew).

6. Outdoor Activities:

6.1 *Hiking and Cycling:* Explore the spectacular natural surroundings by beginning on hiking and cycling paths that give breathtaking views of the vineyards, woodlands, and rolling hills. The Alsace Wine Path provides a lovely path across the region's vineyard-covered countryside.

7. Festivals & Events:

7.1 *Riquewihr Christmas Market:* Experience the romance of the holiday season at the annual Christmas market, when the town comes alive with festive decorations, local crafts, and seasonal delights. The market's pleasant ambiance adds to the village's wonderful attractiveness.

8. Practical Tips:

Best Time to Visit: Spring (April to June) and autumn (September to October) are good times to visit, since the weather is mild, and you can appreciate the splendor of the changing seasons.

Language: While French is the official language, English is often used in tourist areas.

Currency: The currency utilized is the Euro (EUR).

Local Etiquette: It's usual to greet shops and locals with a courteous "Bonjour" before engaging in conversation.

- ## EGUISHEIM

1. **Getting There:**

Riquewihr is conveniently accessible by many kinds of transportation. The closest major airport is Strasbourg Airport, around an hour's drive away. Alternatively, you may take a train to Colmar, which is approximately 20 minutes from Riquewihr, and then utilize local transit or a cab to reach the hamlet.

2. **Housing:**

Riquewihr provides a selection of housing alternatives to suit varied budgets and interests. From quaint boutique hotels to quiet guesthouses, you'll find lots of options that represent the village's typical Alsatian architecture and friendliness.

3. **Exploring the Village:**

3.1 *Historic Old Town:* Stroll through the cobblestone lanes of Riquewihr's ancient old town, surrounded by well-preserved medieval houses embellished with colorful half-timbered facades. The village's layout has remained mostly intact throughout the ages, providing a sensation of going back in time.

3.2 *Musée de la Communication en Alsace:* Visit this fascinating museum to learn about the history of communication and printing in the Alsace area. The museum features diverse instruments, printing machines, and exhibitions that reflect the growth of communication systems.

4. **Wine Tasting:**

4.1 *Alsace Wines:* Riquewihr is located in the heart of Alsace's wine district. Take advantage of the various wine cellars and tasting rooms that provide an opportunity to experience the region's famous white wines, such as Riesling, Gewürztraminer, and Pinot Gris. Learn about the wine-making process and the terroir that gives these wines their special flavor.

5. **Culinary Delights:**

5.1 *Alsatian Cuisine:* Indulge in the delights of Alsatian cuisine in the village's lovely restaurants and cafés. Try typical foods like tarte flambée (a thin, delicious flatbread), choucroute garnie (sauerkraut with sausages and other meats), and baeckeoffe (a substantial meat and vegetable stew).

6. **Outdoor Activities:**

6.1 *Hiking and Cycling:* Explore the spectacular natural surroundings by beginning on hiking and cycling paths that give breathtaking views of the vineyards, woodlands, and rolling hills. The Alsace Wine Path provides a lovely path across the region's vineyard-covered countryside.

7. Festivals & Events:

7.1 Riquewihr Christmas Market: Experience the romance of the holiday season at the annual Christmas market, when the town comes alive with festive decorations, local crafts, and seasonal delights. The market's pleasant ambiance adds to the village's wonderful attractiveness.

8. Practical Tips:

Best Time to Visit: Spring (April to June) and autumn (September to October) are good times to visit, since the weather is mild, and you can appreciate the splendor of the changing seasons.

Language: While French is the official language, English is often used in tourist areas.

Currency: The currency utilized is the Euro (EUR).

Local Etiquette: It's usual to greet shops and locals with a courteous "Bonjour" before engaging in conversation.

• OTHER CHARMING VILLAGES

1. Riquewihr

Located along the Alsace Wine Route, Riquewihr is a fairytale town with cobblestone lanes, beautiful half-timbered buildings, and flower-filled balconies. As you wander around the town, you'll feel like you've gone back in time. Explore the Dolder Tower, a historic gate that gives panoramic views of the hamlet and neighboring vineyards. Don't miss the chance to try local wines and Alsace's famous cuisine at delightful eateries.

2. Eguisheim

Eguisheim is a circular hamlet with concentric streets that spiral around a central castle. This arrangement provides an intimate and warm environment that urges you to explore its small passageways and flower-bedecked nooks. The hamlet is famed for its Alsatian wine production and provides great wine-tasting experiences. The Church of Saint Peter and Saint Paul, with its exquisite architecture, is a must-see.

3. Obernai

Obernai integrates history, culture, and natural beauty flawlessly. Its lovely streets are decorated with colorful residences and pleasant stores. Explore the town's historical landmarks, including the 13th-century Obernai Tower and the Market Square. If you're a history aficionado, visit the Obernai Museum to learn about the region's past. The town's closeness to the Mont Sainte-Odile gives a possibility for spectacular treks.

4. Hunawihr

Nestled between vineyards and encircled by historic defenses, Hunawihr offers a rustic appeal. The fortified church and the stunning castle remains transport you to a bygone period. The area is also home to the Butterfly Garden, a unique attraction that highlights local flora and wildlife. Take a stroll through the vineyards and appreciate the tranquil beauty of the countryside.

5. Kaysersberg

Famous for its Christmas markets and wonderful architecture, Kaysersberg is a jewel in the heart of Alsace. The 16th-century fortified bridge and the stately Château de Kaysersberg are notable sights. The village's rich cultural past may be studied at the Albert Schweitzer Museum. Consider taking a stroll along the Weiss River and appreciating the lovely scenery.

6. Andlau

Andlau is a hidden gem that mixes a medieval ambiance with natural grandeur. The hamlet is notable for its spectacular Saint Peter and Saint-Paul Church and the surrounding Abbey of Andlau.

Surrounded by vineyards and rolling hills, Andlau provides abundant chances for hiking and enjoying the outdoors.

7. Mittelbergheim

With its well-preserved half-timbered buildings and cobblestone lanes, Mittelbergheim is a sanctuary for architectural fans. The town is part of the Alsace Wine Route, giving it a great site to enjoy some of the region's best wines. The village's tiny size adds to its appeal, enabling you to explore it at a leisurely pace.

8. Bergheim

Bergheim's ancient buildings and complete city walls take you back to the middle Ages. Explore the town's walls and gates, such as the Dolder Gate and the Eichwald Tower. The tiny streets are dotted with attractive shops and cafés, presenting a wonderful combination of history and modernity.

CHAPTER 4

MUST-VISIT ATTRACTIONS IN ALSACE

• ALSACE WINE ROUTE

1. **Getting Started:**

Location and Route: The Alsace Wine Route begins in Marlenheim, near Strasbourg, and continues until Thann, close to Mulhouse. The route travels through various villages and towns, including Obernai, Ribeauvillé, and Colmar.

Best Time to Visit: The optimum time to tour the route is between the spring and autumn months when the weather is mild and the vineyards are at their most gorgeous. The harvest season (September to October) is very intriguing.

2. **Exploring the Route:**

Villages & Towns: Each settlement along the road has its particular flavor. Obernai's medieval charm, Riquewihr's fairytale architecture, and Colmar's creative feel are just a few highlights.

Wine Tasting: The Alsace Wine Route is famed for its white wines, including Riesling, Gewürztraminer, and Pinot Gris. Many vineyards provide guided tours and tastings, offering insights into the winemaking process and the region's particular terroir.

Local Cuisine: Don't miss the chance to experience Alsace's gastronomic pleasures, such as tarte flambée (Alsatian pizza), choucroute garnie (sauerkraut with sausages), and kugelhopf (a traditional cake).

3. Cultural and Historical Gems:

Château du Haut-Koenigsbourg: This medieval castle provides panoramic views of the neighboring vineyards and woodlands. It's a beautiful example of Alsatian history and architecture.

Unterlinden Museum: Located in Colmar, this museum has a magnificent collection of art and antiques, including the Isenheim Altarpiece.

Ecomusée d'Alsace: An open-air museum that portrays authentic Alsatian rural life, replete with historical houses, handicrafts, and interactive exhibits.

4. Practical Tips:

Transportation: The path may be explored by automobile, bike, or even on foot. Rental automobiles are available, but be sure to verify local traffic restrictions and parking alternatives.

Accommodation: The communities along the route offer a choice of lodgings, from small bed & breakfasts to luxurious hotels. It's important to book in advance, particularly during high seasons.

Language: While French is the official language, English is frequently used in tourist areas. Learning a few simple French words might improve your experience.

Currency: The Euro (€) is the official unit of exchange.

Responsible Tourism: Respect the environment, local culture, and the privacy of the population. Dispose of rubbish responsibly and follow authorized pathways.

• STRASBOURG CATHEDRAL

1. Historical Significance

Strasbourg Cathedral, created over centuries, is a tribute to the architectural accomplishments of its time. Its foundation goes back to the 11th century, and its building proceeded for many centuries, integrating numerous architectural styles. The cathedral has seen key historical events, making it not simply an architectural marvel but a living testament to the region's history.

2. Architecture and Design

The cathedral's architectural style is largely Gothic, with elements from Romanesque and Renaissance styles. The facade is ornamented with exquisite sculptures, featuring biblical themes and characters. The front includes the renowned astronomical clock and a magnificent rose window. The inside includes awe-inspiring vaulted ceilings, a magnificent nave, and elaborate stained glass windows that reflect multicolored light onto the stone flooring.

3. Astronomical Clock

One of the features of Strasbourg Cathedral is its astronomical clock, a marvel of medieval workmanship. Installed in the 19th century, the clock not only shows time but also displays the location of the planets, the phases of the moon, and several other astronomical facts. Witnessing the clock's hourly procession of figures is a must-see event.

4. Views from the Tower

For a stunning panoramic perspective of Strasbourg and its surroundings, try climbing the cathedral's tower. The climb could be a little tough, but the result is worth it. Gaze over the magnificent half-timbered homes, the flowing River Ill, and the attractive streets of the city below.

5. Practical Information

Location: Place de la Cathédrale, Strasbourg, Alsace, France.

Opening Hours: The cathedral is normally open every day from morning until dusk. The tower has distinct times.

Entry: There is normally no entry price to enter the cathedral, although there can be a fee to visit the tower.

Dress Code: As a place of religion, modest clothes are welcomed.

Guided Tours: Consider attending a guided tour to obtain deeper insights into the cathedral's history and design.

6. Nearby Attractions

While in Strasbourg, discover the city's lovely attractions:

La Petite France: A historic district with lovely waterways, half-timbered buildings, and cobblestone lanes.

Boat Tours: Take a leisurely boat trip through the canals to experience the city from a fresh perspective.

European Parliament: If you're interested in politics and history, the European Parliament is worth a visit.

Museums: Strasbourg features a variety of museums, including the Alsatian Museum and the Strasbourg Museum of Modern and Contemporary Art.

7. Local Cuisine

Indulge in the gastronomic pleasures of Alsace, recognized for its distinctive combination of French and German influences:

Flammekueche: Also known as "tarte flambée," this thin-crust pizza-like dish is covered with cream, onions, and bacon.

Choucroute: A robust meal incorporating sauerkraut, sausages, and other meats.

Alsace Wines: Don't miss the chance to try the region's famed white wines, such as Riesling and Gewürztraminer.

8. Getting There

Strasbourg is well-connected by rail, with high-speed alternatives accessible from major French cities. Strasbourg International Airport also welcomes flights from many European locations.

- ## HAUT-KOENIGSBOURG CASTLE

1. Haut-Koenigsbourg Castle

Haut-Koenigsbourg Castle, commonly referred to as Château du Haut-Koenigsbourg, is a fortified stronghold with roots reaching back to the 12th century. Nestled amid the Vosges Mountains, the castle has experienced centuries of history, changing hands between successive powers and experiencing many architectural alterations.

2. Historical Significance

The castle's history is a tapestry woven with threads of numerous ages. Originally designed as a strategic fortress, it developed to become a symbol of imperial sovereignty under the reign of Emperor Wilhelm II. The castle was substantially renovated in the late 19th and early 20th centuries, showing a combination of medieval and Neo-Romanesque design.

3. Exploring the Castle

3.1 *Architecture and Layout*

Haut-Koenigsbourg's architecture is a witness to both its medieval roots and subsequent improvements. The castle contains reinforced walls, watchtowers, and interior courtyards. Its arrangement enables you to walk into the shoes of its medieval residents and experience life inside its walls.

3.2 *Main Attractions*

Great Hall: This spectacular hall takes you to the grandeur of medieval feasts, replete with historical furnishings and tapestries.

Armory: Explore the collection of weapons, armor, and artillery that offer insight into the military capabilities of the castle's people.

Royal Apartments: Discover the living apartments of the castle's lords and ladies, furnished with historical furniture and décor.

Chapel: A haven of spiritual meditation, the chapel boasts spectacular stained glass windows and delicate woodwork.

4. Practical Information

4.1 *Getting There Haut-Koenigsbourg Castle:* is accessible by automobile and public transit. If driving, follow the instructions and enjoy a picturesque trip to the castle's parking lot. Alternatively, local buses and guided trips are available from adjacent towns.

4.2 *Opening Hours and Admission*

The castle is normally open year-round, with variable hours depending on the season. It's advised to check the official website for the latest updates. Admission fees may apply, with reductions available for students, elders, and families.

4.3 *Guided Tours*

Enhance your experience with guided tours available in several languages. Expert tours give historical context and engaging tales, giving you a greater knowledge of the castle's history.

4.4 *Facilities*

The castle has tourist amenities, including a gift store and a café where you may enjoy local food and drinks while taking in beautiful views.

4.5 *Accessibility*

While the castle's historic history causes obstacles for persons with mobility impairments, attempts have been made to increase accessibility to specific parts. Check the accessibility information before your visit.

5. Nearby Attractions

Extend your Alsatian journey by seeing the picturesque towns, wineries, and other historical sights nearby. The Alsace area is recognized for its beauty and cultural richness

- ## PETITE FRANCE

1. Haut-Petite France

Location: Haut-Petite France is located in the northeastern portion of France, bordering Germany and Switzerland. It's recognized for its picturesque towns, vineyard-covered landscapes, and rich history inspired by both French and German cultures.

2. Getting There By Air:

The nearest major airports are Strasbourg International Airport and EuroAirport Basel-Mulhouse-Freiburg. Both provide links to many European cities.

By rail: The TGV (high-speed rail) links Strasbourg to major cities like Paris, Frankfurt, and Zurich, making it easy for international tourists.

3. Accommodation

Haut-Petite France provides a selection of lodgings, from boutique hotels to quaint guesthouses. Strasbourg, the capital of Alsace, provides a range of alternatives to pick from. For a more immersive experience, try staying in a classic Alsatian timber-framed home.

4. Things to Do Explore Strasbourg

Strasbourg Cathedral: A marvel of Gothic design, this cathedral has complex decorations and gives panoramic views from its tower.

La Petite France: Wander around the lovely neighborhood of La Petite France, famed for its half-timbered buildings, canals, and cobblestone lanes.

European Parliament: Take a guided tour to learn about the European Union's workings at one of its key seats.

Discover Alsatian Villages Riquewihr: This well-preserved medieval hamlet is noted for its colorful buildings, cobblestone streets, and local wines.

Colmar: Known as the "Little Venice" of Alsace, Colmar's canals and flower-filled alleyways create a magical environment.

Eguisheim: Explore this round hamlet with concentric streets, bright flowers, and a center castle.

Experience Cuisine

Tarte Flambée: Also called Flammekueche, this thin, crispy pizza-like dish is a local delicacy topped with different things including cheese, onions, and bacon.

Choucroute: A substantial meal incorporating sauerkraut and other sorts of sausages and meats.

Alsace Wines: Taste the region's superb white wines, including Riesling, Gewürztraminer, and Pinot Gris.

5. Outdoor Activities

The Wine Route

Embark on the Alsace Wine Route, a picturesque excursion through vineyards, towns, and wineries. Sample wines, learn about the winemaking process, and enjoy gorgeous surroundings.

Hiking and Cycling Haut-Petite France has several pathways for hikers and cyclists, ranging from peaceful strolls to strenuous hikes. The Vosges Mountains offer a stunning background for outdoor enthusiasts.

6. Cultural Experiences Museums:

Discover the history and cultural legacy of the Alsace area via exhibitions, relics, and interactive displays.

Museum of Contemporary and Contemporary Art: Located in Strasbourg, this museum shows a varied collection of contemporary artworks.

Festivals

Strasbourg Christmas Market: Experience the romance of the holiday season with one of Europe's oldest and most picturesque Christmas markets.

Alsace Wine Festivals: Celebrate the local wine culture at numerous festivals throughout the year, involving tastings, music, and traditional dances.

7. *Practical Information Language:* French and Alsatian dialects. English is spoken in most tourist locations.

Currency: Euro (€)

Time Zone: Central European Time (CET)

Local Etiquette: Greet with "Bonjour" (Good morning) and "Bonsoir" (Good evening). Punctuality is valued.

- ## UNTERLINDEN MUSEUM

1. History:

The Unterlinden Museum is situated in the center of Colmar, a lovely Alsatian town. It was first created in the 19th century in a former Dominican monastery. The museum's name, "Unterlinden," translates to "under the linden trees," commemorating the enormous linden trees that decorate the museum's courtyard.

The museum earned worldwide praise after its substantial refurbishment and expansion in 2015. The historic center is paired with contemporary architectural components, producing a distinctive combination of old and new. This combination matches the broad collection contained inside, which extends from antiquity to current art.

2. Notable Artworks:

The Unterlinden Museum features an amazing collection that appeals to a broad spectrum of creative inclinations. Some of the significant artworks include:

Isenheim Altarpiece: Created by Matthias Grünewald, this 16th-century masterwork is a crucial piece of Christian art. Its ornate panels represent themes of Christ's death and resurrection, as well as the suffering of St. Anthony.

The Virgin and Child by the Fireside: Painted by the famous artist Martin Schongauer, this artwork conveys a calm household setting that oozes warmth and tenderness.

Modern Art Collection: The museum's collection isn't restricted to historical artifacts. It also offers a variety of contemporary artworks by artists including Marc Chagall, Salvador Dalí, and Max Ernst.

3. Visitor Information:

Opening Hours: The museum is normally open from 9:00 AM to 6:00 PM. However, it's essential to check the official website for any updates or changes to the operating hours.

Entry Fees: The entry charge varies dependent on age, with reductions available for students, the elderly, and organizations. Admission is typically free for those under a specific age or for certain events.

Guided Tours: To obtain a greater knowledge of the artworks and their historical context, try attending a guided tour. These excursions are frequently accessible in various languages and give significant information.

4. **Practical Tips:**

Organize Ahead: Given the museum's popularity, it's a good idea to organize your visit in advance. Consider buying tickets online to avoid lengthy waits.

Photography: Photography rules vary, so make careful to verify whether photography is permitted in the particular exhibits you're interested in.

Acceptable Attire: As a location of cultural and historical importance, it's acceptable to dress modestly while visiting the museum.

• EUROPA-PARK

1. Europa-Park Alsace

Europa-Park: Europa-Park is a world-class theme park situated in Rust, Germany, on the border with France. It encompasses an area of 95 hectares and is separated into 18 themed zones, each representing a different European nation. The park provides an astounding array of activities, events, and entertainment opportunities for guests of all ages.

Alsace Region: Situated in northeastern France, Alsace is recognized for its picturesque towns, wineries, and rich cultural history. The region's distinctive combination of French and German influences is evident in its food, architecture, and customs.

2. Getting There By Air:

The closest major airports are Strasbourg Airport (SXB) and EuroAirport Basel Mulhouse Freiburg (BSL/MLH/EAP). Both provide strong connections to major European cities.

By railway: The Freiburg im Breisgau railway station in Germany is well-connected to Rust, where Europa Park is situated. From there, you may take a local rail or bus to the park.

By automobile: Europa-Park is readily accessible by automobile, with well-marked highways from major adjacent cities. There is free parking available in the park.

3. Accommodation On-Site Hotels:

Europa-Park provides a selection of themed hotels for a comprehensive experience. Choose from the Mediterranean-themed Hotel Colosseo, the rustic Hotel Bell Rock, or the adventurous Camp Resort, among others.

Off-Site Hotels: Several hotels and guesthouses in Rust and adjacent towns cater to different budgets and interests.

4. Attractions

Themed zones: Explore the meticulously constructed themed zones, such as Italy, France, Spain, and more. Each section includes rides, entertainment, and eateries that embody the character of the various nations.

Rides: Europa-Park features a broad choice of rides, from exciting roller coasters like Silver Star and Blue Fire to family-friendly attractions like Arthur – In the Minimoys Kingdom and Pirates in Batavia.

Concerts & Entertainment: Don't miss out on the enthralling live concerts, musicals, and parades that take place throughout the day. The Europa-Park Theater provides amazing shows.

5. Dining and Cuisine

European gastronomic delights: Experience the gastronomic variety of Europe via the numerous eateries in Europa Park. Sample German sausages, Italian spaghetti, French croissants, and more.

Special Dining Experiences: Some restaurants provide character dining experiences where you may meet Europa-Park mascots and characters.

6. Practical Tips

Park Opening Hours: Europa-Park's opening hours fluctuate throughout the year, so check the official website for up-to-date information.

Tickets: Purchase tickets online to avoid huge waits at the door.

Weather: Alsace has a moderate climate. Pack appropriately, particularly if you intend to come during cooler months.

Language: French and German are the predominant languages spoken in the area. English is generally understood in tourist regions.

ALSACE TRAVEL GUIDE 2023-2024

CHAPTER 5

OUTDOOR ACTIVITIES IN ALSACE

• HIKING AND NATURE TRAILS

Hiking Essentials

Before you head out on your hiking excursion in Alsace, it's necessary to be prepared. Here are some elements to consider:

1. **Proper Footwear**

Invest in a decent pair of hiking boots or robust walking shoes. The trails in Alsace might vary in terrain, so wearing comfortable and supportive footwear is vital.

2. **Appropriate Clothing**

Dress in layers, since weather conditions might change swiftly. A moisture-wicking base layer, a warm insulating layer, and a waterproof upper layer are advised. Don't forget a hat, gloves, and sunglasses for sun protection.

3. **Trail Maps and Navigation**

While some trails are well-marked, it's always a good idea to bring a thorough trail map or use a navigation program on your smartphone. This will help you keep on track and prevent getting lost.

4. Hydration and Snacks

Carry enough amount of water to remain hydrated during your trek. Pack energy-boosting foods like almonds, granola bars, and fruits to keep your energy levels up.

5. First Aid Kit

A simple first aid pack containing necessities like bandages, disinfectant wipes, and pain medicines may be a lifesaver in case of minor accidents.

Top Hiking and Nature Trails in Alsace

1. The Grand Ballon Trail

The Grand Ballon Trail is a tough path that leads you to the highest mountain in the Vosges Mountains, Grand Ballon. The walk provides amazing panoramic views of the surrounding landscapes, including vineyards, woodlands, and attractive towns. This path is intended for experienced hikers owing to its severe ascents and descents.

2. The Wine Route Nature Trail

For a more leisurely encounter, the Wine Route Nature Trail is a terrific alternative. This walk runs past vineyards, enabling you to immerse yourself in Alsace's wine culture. Along the route, you'll get the chance to visit vineyards, sample local wines, and enjoy the gorgeous rural views.

3. The Château du Haut-Koenigsbourg Trail

This walk leads to the historic Château du Haut-Kœnigsbourg, a medieval castle that looks into Alsace's past. The trek takes you through beautiful woodlands and picturesque towns before finishing at the spectacular castle itself. The panoramic views from the castle's ramparts are a highlight of this walk.

4. The Petite Camargue Alsacienne Nature Reserve

If you're a wildlife fan, the Petite Camargue Alsacienne Wildlife Reserve is a must-visit. This marsh region is home to varied bird species and distinctive plants. Wooden boardwalks and viewing spots make it simple to tour the area without damaging the sensitive ecology.

5. The Munster Valley Trail

For a blend of natural beauty and cultural encounters, the Munster Valley Trail is a good option. This walk takes you through the Munster Valley, noted for its beautiful meadows and medieval towns. You'll also get the chance to try Munster Cheese, a local specialty.

• CYCLING ROUTES

1. Alsace

Alsace is a region noted for its unique combination of French and German influences. With its unique architecture, bustling cities, and the background of the Vosges Mountains, Alsace is an enticing environment for bicycle aficionados. The region's well-maintained roads, a vast network of bike trails, and beautiful routes make it a perfect place for a riding journey.

2. Planning your Cycling Trip

2.1 *Best Time to Visit*

The greatest time to explore Alsace on two wheels is during the spring and summer months (May to September). The weather is often nice, and you may experience the full grandeur of the region's scenery.

2.2 *Rental and Equipment*

There is no need to worry if you lack a bicycle. Alsace provides various bike rental outlets where you may select a perfect ride for your excursion. Make sure to enquire about rental restrictions, equipment availability, and any needed reservations.

2.3 *Accommodation*

Alsace boasts a range of lodging alternatives, from quaint guesthouses to upscale hotels. Many facilities are cyclist-friendly, providing safe storage for bikes and equipment for basic repairs.

2.4 *Safety and Regulations*

Familiarize yourself with French traffic restrictions and cycling laws before going on your tour. Always wear a helmet, respect traffic regulations, and keep visible to other road users.

3. **Noteworthy Cycling Routes and Trails**

3.1 *Route des Vins d'Alsace*

One of the most famous bicycle routes, the Route des Vins d'Alsace, takes you into the heart of Alsace's famed wineries. As you ride along this gorgeous path, you'll have the opportunity to explore lovely towns like Riquewihr, Ribeauvillé, and Eguisheim, each giving a taste of Alsace's rich culture and history.

3.2 *Vosges Mountains Circuit*

For the most ambitious riders, the Vosges Mountains Circuit provides tough climbs and satisfying descents. This path takes you through lush woods, alpine meadows, and tranquil lakes, affording spectacular panoramic views along the way.

3.3 *Rhine River Cycling Path*

Following the route of the Rhine River, this trail provides a calm and family-friendly riding experience. You'll have the chance to visit Alsace's bigger cities, such as Strasbourg and Colmar while enjoying the calm riverbank beauty.

3.4 *Alsace Wine Route*

Cycling the Alsace Wine Route exposes you to the region's viticultural heritage. This route twists through vineyard-covered hills, giving breathtaking panoramas and the opportunity to drink some of Alsace's best wines at local wineries.

4. **Practical Tips and Recommendations**

4.1 *Navigation*

Bring a thorough map or GPS gadget to assist navigate Alsace's bicycle routes properly. Many roads are well-marked, but having a backup navigation gadget is usually a smart idea.

4.2 *Hydration and Nutrition*

Stay well-hydrated and energetic on your rides by packing extra water and food. Alsace's villages typically offer lovely cafés where you may recharge with local pleasures.

4.3 *Cultural Etiquette*

Respect the local culture by obeying traditions and being cautious of noise levels, particularly while driving through villages.

4.4 *Bike Maintenance*

Carry basic tools and supplies for modest bike maintenance. It's also advisable to have a list of bike repair shops along your preferred routes, just in case.

• WATER SPORTS AND RIVER CRUISES

1. Water Sports:

1.1 *Canoeing and Kayaking:* The many rivers and water bodies in Alsace make it a perfect location for canoeing and kayaking lovers. The Ill River and the Fecht River provide quiet and picturesque paths appropriate for novices, while the more daring may take on the trials of the Thur River's rapids. Local outfitters offer equipment rental and guided trips for all ability levels.

1.2 *Stand-Up Paddleboarding (SUP):* SUP aficionados may enjoy gliding over the peaceful waters of Alsace's lakes and rivers. Lac Blanc and Lac de Gérardmer provide lovely settings for relaxed paddleboarding sessions. These places also give SUP instructions for novices to help them balance and negotiate the water with ease.

1.3 *Windsurfing and Kitesurfing:*

For those seeking more adventurous water activities, Alsace's windswept lakes, notably Lac du Der-Chantecoq, are popular places for windsurfing and kitesurfing. The consistent winds and spacious oceans offer the ideal circumstances for aficionados of these adrenaline-pumping pastimes.

2. **River Cruises:**

2.1 *The Rhine River Cruises:* The Rhine River, which forms the eastern boundary of Alsace, provides a stunning background for river cruises. From Strasbourg, you may begin on a leisurely cruise that takes you past gorgeous towns, vineyards, and old castles. The voyage also gives a unique view of the region's cultural variety.

2.2 *Canal Cruises:* Alsace's complicated network of canals, such as the Canal du Rhône au Rhin, gives a chance for quiet and lovely cruises. Travel through the heart of Alsace's wine region and discover beautiful towns, such as Eguisheim and Riquewihr, along the route. These cruises frequently feature wine tastings and local food, delivering a full flavor of Alsace's gastronomic history.

2.3 *Ill River Cruises in Strasbourg:* Discover the attractive city of Strasbourg from a fresh viewpoint with a cruise down the Ill River. Drift beneath picturesque bridges and through old timber-framed homes as you learn about the city's rich history and architectural wonders. Sunset cruises give especially lovely views of Strasbourg's lit attractions.

3. **Practical Information:**

3.1 *Best Time to Visit:*

The greatest season for water activities and river excursions in Alsace is during the warmer months, from May to September when the weather is good and water temperatures are more tempting.

3.2 *Equipment and Rentals*: Most water sports equipment may be hired from local outfitters, who also offer safety gear and lessons for novices. For river cruises, several tour providers offer guided excursions, frequently incorporating instructive commentary in multiple languages.

3.3 *Safety Precautions*: While partaking in water activities, always follow safety requirements and carry proper gear, such as life jackets. Follow the directions of guides and specialists, especially if you're new to the activity.

• SKIING AND WATER SPORTS

Skiing in Alsace

1. **Ski Resorts:** Alsace features multiple ski resorts that cater to all ability levels, making it a perfect location for both novices and expert skiers. Popular ski resorts include:

Le Lac Blanc: Situated in the Vosges Mountains, Le Lac Blanc provides breathtaking panoramic views and a selection of ski slopes appropriate for all abilities.

Le Champ du Feu: Known for its family-friendly ambiance, Le Champ du Feu boasts mild slopes excellent for beginners and intermediate skiers.

Markstein: This resort is recognized for its diversified terrain and outstanding cross-country skiing chances.

2. **Skiing Opportunities:** Alsace's ski resorts give a choice of skiing options:

Alpine Skiing: Experience the excitement of slicing down well-groomed slopes of varied difficulty levels.

Cross-Country Skiing: Explore the quiet winter scenery on cross-country paths that run through woods and meadows.

Snowboarding: Many resorts provide snowboarding facilities with specific places for snowboarders to practice tricks and jump.

3. **Ski Schools and Equipment Rental:** If you're new to skiing, worry not! Ski schools in Alsace provide instruction for all ages and ability levels. Rental stores offer top-quality ski equipment and gear, ensuring you have a safe and pleasurable day on the slopes.

Water Sports in Alsace

1. **Strasbourg waterways**: Explore the heart of Strasbourg via its fascinating network of waterways. Join guided boat cruises to experience the city's ancient architecture and attractive districts from a fresh viewpoint.

2. **Rhine River Adventures**: The Rhine River provides many water-based activities:

Kayaking & Canoeing: Paddle down the Rhine's quiet sections, soaking in the gorgeous landscape and enjoying a relaxing experience.

Boat Cruises: Hop onboard a river tour to view Alsace's scenery and towns from the luxury of a leisurely boat ride.

3. **Lac de Gérardmer:** This gorgeous lake in the Vosges Mountains is a sanctuary for water sports enthusiasts:

Swimming: Enjoy a pleasant swim in the crystalline waters of Lac de Gérardmer during the warmer months.

Sailing and Windsurfing: Rent equipment and glide over the lake's surface, driven by the calm wind.

Fishing: Engage in the quiet art of fishing while surrounded by the serene beauty of the lake and mountains.

Travel Tips

1. **Weather Considerations:** For skiing, visit Alsace during the winter months (December to February) when the snow-covered landscapes are at their finest. For water sports, plan your vacation in the warmer months (May to September) when temperatures are more suited for aquatic activities.

2. **Accommodation:** Alsace provides a selection of hotels, from modest chalets in ski areas to beautiful guesthouses along the canals. Book in advance, particularly during high seasons.

3. **Cuisine and Culture:** Indulge in Alsace's famous gastronomic scene. Sample typical foods like choucroute (sauerkraut with sausages) and tarte flambée (a sort of thin pizza). Immerse yourself in Alsace's rich culture by touring its medieval villages and historic attractions.

4. **Safety Precautions:** Whether skiing or enjoying water activities, always emphasize safety. Follow standards, use suitable clothing, and keep informed about weather conditions.

ALSACE TRAVEL GUIDE 2023-2024

CHAPTER 6

ALSACE'S CULINARY DELIGHTS

- ### TRADITIONAL ALSATIAN CUISINE

Sauerkraut (Choucroute): A traditional Alsatian cuisine, sauerkraut consists of fermented cabbage slow-cooked with different meats including sausages, pig, and ham. It reflects the German influence on the cuisine and is a hearty comfort meal.

Tarte Flambée (Flammekueche): Often referred to as "Alsatian pizza," this thin-crust pastry is covered with crème fraîche, onions, and bacon. It's a delicious pleasure that tantalizes the taste buds.

Baeckeoffe: This dish displays the French aspect of Alsatian cuisine. Baeckeoffe is a dish prepared with marinated meats (typically lamb, hog, and beef), potatoes, onions, and fragrant herbs, slow-cooked to perfection.

Kugelhopf: A classic Alsatian treat, Kugelhopf is a sweet, yeast-based cake generally flavored with almonds and raisins. It's a classic for Christmas gatherings and shows the region's baking skills.

Alsace Wines: Alsace is famed for its superb white wines, such as Riesling, Gewürztraminer, and Pinot Gris. These wines nicely complement Alsatian meals and give a particular flavor to the region's vineyards.

• FAMOUS ALSATIAN DISHES

1. **Choucroute Garnie:** Choucroute Garnie is undoubtedly the most emblematic dish of Alsace. This savory meal comprises finely fermented sauerkraut, slow-cooked to perfection, and decorated with a variety of delectable meats, such as sausages, pork chops, and ham. The tastes merge in a perfect symphony, delivering a fulfilling dinner that represents the region's cultural fusion.

2. **Tarte Flambée (Flammekueche):** Tarte Flambée, sometimes referred to as Flammekueche, is a rustic flatbread pleasure that resembles a thin-crust pizza. A paper-thin dough is topped with crème fraîche, onions, and bacon. The combination of the crunchy crust, creamy crème fraîche, and smokey bacon results in a delicious juxtaposition of textures and sensations.

3. **Baeckeoffe:** Baeckeoffe is a cozy casserole meal that comprises layers of marinated meats, including lamb, beef, and hog, mixed with sliced potatoes, onions, and fragrant herbs. This delectable combination is slow-cooked in a white wine broth, enabling the ingredients to mingle and integrate, producing a meal that's both substantial and fragrant.

4. **Coq au Riesling:** Similar to the classic French meal Coq au Vin, Coq au Riesling is a regional version that swaps red wine with the famed Alsatian white wine, Riesling. Tender chicken pieces are cooked to perfection in a subtle Riesling sauce, accented with

mushrooms, onions, and fresh herbs. The outcome is a meal that's both gorgeous and soul-warming.

5. **Kougelhopf:** No Alsatian dinner is complete without a taste of Kougelhopf, a classic brioche-like cake that's popular as a dessert or morning delight. The dough is supplemented with butter, almonds, raisins, and a dash of Kirsch (cherry brandy), which lends a wonderful taste. The cake is cooked in a characteristic fluted shape, resulting in an invitingly scented and aesthetically beautiful delicacy.

6. **Munster Cheese:** Munster Cheese, named after the Vosges Mountains in Alsace, is a pungent and creamy cheese that's a cornerstone of Alsatian cuisine. This washed-rind cheese has a powerful taste profile with earthy and sour overtones. It's commonly served with bread, along with a glass of Alsatian white wine, and may also be included in numerous recipes.

7. **Alsatian Wine**: Alsace is recognized for its superb wines, notably its white wines. The region's terroir and cold temperature lead to the development of high-quality varietals such as Riesling, Gewürztraminer, and Pinot Gris. Visitors get the chance to visit the local vineyards, indulge in wine tastings, and learn about the winemaking process, making it an integral component of an Alsatian gastronomic adventure.

• LOCAL WINES AND VINEYARD

1. Alsace Wines: A Blend of Tradition and Innovation

Alsace is recognized for producing some of the best white wines in the world. The region's winemaking legacy extends back generations, with an emphasis on conserving traditional processes while embracing innovations. The Alsatian winemakers take pleasure in making wines that represent the region's specific terroir and highlight the individuality of each grape type.

2. Terroir: The Essence of Alsace Wines

The soil of Alsace plays a crucial role in determining the flavor of its wines. The area is defined by its distinct microclimate, which is affected by the Vosges Mountains to the west and the Rhine River to the east. The combination of cold temperatures, plentiful sunlight, and different soil types adds to the delicate aromas and flavors found in Alsace wines.

3. Grape Varieties: Diversity in Every Sip

Alsace is famous for its concentration on single-varietal wines, enabling the individual traits of each grape type to show. Key grape varietals include:

Riesling: Known for its fragrant strength and bright acidity, Alsace Riesling wines vary from bone-dry to somewhat sweet, presenting a variety of flavors from citrus to stone fruit.

Gewürztraminer: This fragrant grape variety yields wines with exotic floral aromas, lychee, and spice. Often off-dry or sweet, Gewürztraminer wines are a real sensory experience.

Pinot Gris: Alsace Pinot Gris wines are rich and full-bodied, having notes of luscious orchard fruits and a tinge of smokiness.

Pinot Blanc: A versatile and accessible varietal, Pinot Blanc provides fresh and easy-drinking wines, suitable for complementing regional food.

Muscat: Whether dry or somewhat sweet, Muscat wines fascinate with their flowery and grapey scents, making them stand out among Alsace's offers.

4. Exploring the Vineyards of Alsace

4.1 *Route des Vins d'Alsace (Alsace Wine Route)*

Embark on a tour through the famed Alsace Wine Route, weaving past scenic towns, rolling vineyards, and lovely wineries. This 170-kilometer trip gives the chance to visit famous winemaking communities such as Riquewihr, Ribeauvillé, and Eguisheim. Explore family-owned vineyards, sample tastings, and learn about the winemaking process firsthand.

4.2 *Vineyard Tours and Tastings*

Delve into the heart of Alsace's wine culture by participating in vineyard tours and tastings. Many wineries encourage tourists to view their estates, vineyards, and cellars, offering insights into the workmanship behind each bottle. Engage with enthusiastic winemakers as they share their skills and love for winemaking.

5. Food and Wine Pairing: The Alsatian Gastronomic Experience

Pairing Alsace wines with local food is a joy for the senses. Traditional Alsatian foods such as choucroute garnie (sauerkraut with sausages and meats), tarte flambée (a thin, savory flatbread), and coq au Riesling (chicken cooked in Riesling wine) compliment the wines' tastes. The region's fragrant and rich wines improve the dining experience, providing harmonic pairings that highlight both cuisine and wine.

6. Annual Wine Festivals and Events

Experience the colorful culture of Alsace via its various wine festivals and events. The Alsace Wine Fair in Colmar is a highlight, delivering an entire journey into the region's wine culture. The festival gives the opportunity to sample a broad selection of wines, meet winemakers, and partake in activities that commemorate the art of winemaking.

7. Sustainable Winemaking in Alsace

Many wineries in Alsace are devoted to sustainable and eco-friendly winemaking processes. Learn about efforts like organic and biodynamic viticulture, which seek to maintain the region's distinctive terroir for future generations while producing high-quality wines with little environmental effect.

8. Bringing Alsace Wines Home

No vacation to Alsace would be complete without taking home a couple of bottles of your favorite wines. Explore local wine stores and markets to uncover an assortment of Alsace wines that fit your palette, whether it's a crisp Riesling, a fragrant Gewürztraminer, or a rich Pinot Gris.

FOOD FESTIVALS AND MARKETS

Food Festivals and Markets

1. Alsace Wine Route Festival

Location: Various villages along the Alsace Wine Route

Timing: August-October

Discover Alsace's world-famous wines at this yearly event. The Wine Route spans picturesque communities, providing wine tastings, cellar tours, and food pairings. Savor the region's Riesling, Gewürztraminer, and Pinot Gris, accompanied by local cheeses and charcuterie.

2. Strasbourg Christmas Market Location: Strasbourg

Timing: Late November-December

Immerse yourself in the wonderful Strasbourg Christmas Market, one of the oldest and most recognizable in Europe. Indulge in hot mulled wine, gingerbread, and regional pastries while browsing wooden kiosks decked with decorations, crafts, and local delicacies.

3. Foire aux Vins d'Alsace

Location: Colmar

Timing: August-September

Colmar holds the Alsace Wine Fair, highlighting the region's vineyards. Sample a varied choice of wines, attend wine seminars, and enjoy music and exhibits. Local dishes like tarte flambée and choucroute garnie contribute to the joyful ambiance.

4. Obernai Traditional Market Location: Obernai

Timing: Every Thursday

Experience Alsace's everyday life at the historic market in Obernai. Local farmers and artists converge to offer fresh vegetables, cheeses, meats, and crafts. Engage with people, try regional dishes, and absorb the colorful ambiance of this quaint town.

5. Fête de la Quiche

Location: Niedermorschwihr

Timing: May

Celebrate the popular quiche Lorraine in the hamlet of Niedermorschwihr. This event pays tribute to the renowned dish with quiche-making contests, tastings, and cultural activities. Experience the creativity behind this famous savory dish.

ALSACE TRAVEL GUIDE 2023-2024

CHAPTER 7

ACCOMMODATION OPTIONS IN ALSACE

- ### LUXURY HOTELS AND RESORTS

1. Château de l'Ile - Strasbourg

Nestled on a secluded island along the Ill River, Château de l'Ile provides a magnificent refuge amid Strasbourg. This 19th-century castle-turned-hotel features exquisite rooms and suites filled with antique antiques and contemporary conveniences.

The magnificent Michelin-starred restaurant, L'Auberge de l'Ill, delivers gourmet French cuisine with an emphasis on local ingredients. Relax in the spa, enjoy a leisurely walk on the lovely grounds, or explore the historic city center only a short drive away.

2. Hôtel Les Haras - Strasbourg

A blend of contemporary style and vintage charm, Hôtel Les Haras is housed in a former 18th-century stud farm. The rooms and suites are attractively decorated with modern designs and provide views of the city or the hotel's courtyard. Indulge in a gourmet adventure at the hotel's restaurant, presenting inventive Alsatian cuisine. The central position offers easy discovery of Strasbourg's renowned sights, including the Cathedral and La Petite France area.

3. La Cheneaudière & Spa - Colroy-la-Roche

Tucked hidden in the beautiful Alsatian woodland, La Cheneaudière & Spa is a sanctuary of tranquillity and elegance. The rooms and suites provide a warm and sophisticated ambiance, while the spa is a refuge for relaxation and regeneration. Indulge in gourmet meals at the hotel's restaurant, which emphasizes fresh and locally-sourced products. The surrounding countryside welcomes you to explore hiking paths, while the adjacent Alsace Wine Route is a pleasure for wine connoisseurs.

4. Hôtel Le Parc - Obernai

Situated in the lovely village of Obernai, Hôtel Le Parc blends luxury with Alsatian originality. The rooms and suites are elegantly designed, and the hotel's Michelin-starred restaurant, Le Parc, delivers exquisite meals produced by talented chefs. Unwind in the spa or take a swim in the outdoor pool among gorgeous flowers. The hotel's closeness to Obernai's historic town provides a great cultural experience.

5. Villa René Lalique - Wingen-sur-Moder

For a truly delightful vacation, Villa René Lalique provides a combination of art, elegance, and food. This 5-star hotel has specially designed rooms and suites, each displaying Lalique's exceptional workmanship. The two-Michelin-starred restaurant, headed by Chef Jean-Georges Klein, offers an excellent dining experience. Don't miss the chance to see the Lalique Museum nearby, showing the famed glassmaker's masterpieces.

6. Les Violettes Hotel & Spa - Jungholtz

Nestled in the foothills of the Vosges Mountains, Les Violettes Hotel & Spa provides stunning vistas and elegant luxury. The rooms and suites are attractively equipped, and the spa offers a selection of treatments and relaxing experiences. Indulge in Alsatian gastronomic delights in the hotel's restaurant, accompanied by an excellent wine selection. The position enables one for visiting surrounding hiking trails and attractive communities.

7. Hôtel Cour du Corbeau - Strasbourg

Immerse yourself in history at Hôtel Cour du Corbeau, a beautiful 16th-century chateau in the center of Strasbourg. The rooms and suites mix antique elegance with contemporary comforts. Explore the bustling city on foot, seeing landmarks such as the Kammerzell House and Strasbourg Cathedral. After a day of sightseeing, return to the hotel's pleasant ambiance and indulge in French cuisine at the on-site restaurant.

8. Hôtel Les Sources des Alpes - Leukerbad

While officially situated in Switzerland, Hôtel Les Sources des Alpes is worth the small trip from Alsace. Set in the lovely mountain village of Leukerbad, this luxury hotel provides thermal spa experiences and stunning alpine views. The attractively constructed rooms and suites give comfort and elegance. Indulge in the therapeutic pleasures of the thermal baths, and eat exquisite meals in the hotel's restaurant.

• CHARMING BED AND BREAKFASTS

1. Discovering Alsace: A Whirlwind of Beauty and Culture

Nestled in the northeastern corner of France, Alsace is recognized for its particular combination of French and German influences. The area is noted for its fairy-tale towns, cobblestone alleys, half-timbered buildings covered with bright flowers, and the breathtaking background of the Vosges Mountains. Alsace possesses a rich past, apparent in its architecture, culture, and gastronomy. Visitors may visit historic castles, enjoy wine sampling in world-class vineyards, and immerse themselves in the cultural tapestry of the region.

2. The Allure of Bed and Breakfasts

When visiting Alsace, one of the greatest ways to properly enjoy the region's charm and warmth is by staying in a bed & breakfast. Unlike standard hotels, bed & breakfasts provide a more customized and intimate experience. Hosts frequently offer their homes to tourists, giving a pleasant environment and insider insights into local sites and activities.

Guests may sample handmade breakfasts utilizing local foods and enjoy the comfort of specially furnished rooms that reflect the region's distinct character.

3. Top Charming Bed and Breakfasts in Alsace

La Maison d'Alsace, Strasbourg: This historic B&B is situated in the center of Strasbourg, enabling visitors to conveniently explore the city's famed cathedral, canals, and lovely districts. With its exquisite accommodations and closeness to cultural sites, La Maison d'Alsace provides a perfect combination of elegance and ease.

Le Petit Château, Ribeauvillé: Set against the background of vineyards and rolling hills, this B&B resembles a beautiful small castle. Guests may enjoy panoramic views, relax in the beautiful garden, and appreciate the tranquillity of the Alsace countryside.

Maison des Rêves, Colmar: Known for its fairy-tale ambiance, Colmar is home to the charming Maison des Rêves. This B&B embodies the spirit of the town's charm, with its timber-framed building and comfortable rooms, making it a great base for exploring Colmar's cobblestone streets and canals.

Au Coeur de l'Alsace, Obernai: A combination of rustic charm and contemporary luxury, this B&B in Obernai gives a warm welcome to tourists. Situated in a town noted for its medieval architecture and Alsatian customs, visitors may experience a combination of history and tranquility.

4. Making the Most of Your Stay

While staying in a delightful bed and breakfast in Alsace, take advantage of the unique experiences the area has to offer:

Explore the Alsace Wine Route and enjoy wine tastings at famous vineyards.

Wander through the fairytale town of Eguisheim, noted for its flower-decked lanes and medieval charm.

Visit the Strasbourg Christmas Market, one of the oldest and most charming Christmas markets in Europe.

Sample typical Alsatian meals such as tarte flambée and choucroute garnie at local restaurants.

5. Embrace the Enchantment

Alsace's beauty and cultural legacy make it a location that makes a lasting impact. By choosing to stay in a lovely bed and breakfast, you'll immerse yourself in the region's warm hospitality and create memories that capture the essence of Alsace's attraction.

● BUDGET-FRIENDLY ACCOMMODATIONS

1. Guesthouses and Bed & Breakfasts

Guesthouses and Bed & Breakfasts (B&Bs) are popular alternatives for budget-conscious vacationers. These hotels give a warm and unique experience while enabling you to interact with local hosts. Many B&Bs in Alsace are housed in classic half-timbered homes, lending to the region's particular character.

Advantages:

Personalized service and local insights from hosts.

Typically situated in attractive towns or rural surroundings.

Affordable prices that frequently include breakfast.

Tips:

Make reservations in advance, especially during peak tourist seasons.

Look for guesthouses with shared amenities to cut expenses.

Read reviews to guarantee a great experience.

2. Hostels

Alsace also provides several hostels, notably in bigger towns and cities like Strasbourg and Colmar. Hostels offer a social environment and are great for single travelers or those wishing to meet other adventures.

Advantages:

Budget-friendly dormitory-style accommodation.

Communal places for mingling and meeting other tourists.

Some hostels provide individual rooms for couples or families.

Tips:

Check the amenities and evaluations to guarantee cleanliness and security.

Look for hostels with kitchens to save money on meals.

Consider the location's closeness to public transit and attractions.

3. Vacation Rentals and Apartments

Renting a holiday apartment may be a good alternative for budget tourists, particularly for longer stays or groups. Having your kitchen might also help you save money on eating out.

Advantages:

More room and privacy compared to regular hotels.

Kitchen amenities for cooking your meals.

Economical for groups or families vacationing together.

Tips:

Research the area to verify it's well-connected and safe.

Check for extra expenses, like cleaning charges or security deposits.

Look for flats with reasonable cancellation policies.

4. Camping and Campsites

For the adventurous visitor, camping may be an interesting and budget-friendly choice in Alsace. The area provides different campsites with amenities that cater to both tent and camper van camping.

Advantages:

Close closeness to nature and outdoor activities.

Affordable prices for campgrounds.

Opportunity to experience Alsace's magnificent scenery.

Tips:

Pack adequate camping supplies for the season.

Research campgrounds in advance and make bookings if required.

Be careful of camping restrictions and regulations.

5. Budget-Friendly Hotels

While Alsace is famed for its lovely guesthouses and inns, there are other budget-friendly hotel alternatives available. Look for motels that provide basic facilities at cheap costs.

Advantages:

Convenient locations, frequently near town centers.

Standard facilities such as private bathrooms and Wi-Fi.

Competitive rates for budget-conscious tourists.

Tips:

Read reviews to guarantee cleanliness and comfort.

Consider motels just outside main tourist destinations for better prices.

Look for package offers that include breakfast or other amenities.

• UNIQUE STAYS: CASTLE AND VINEYARD LODGINGS

1. Castle Lodgings

1.1 *Château de Haut-Koenigsbourg*

Perched on a hilltop, Château du Haut-Kœnigsbourg is a medieval fortress that looks into Alsace's history. Visitors may stay in accommodations that mix historical ambiance with contemporary amenities. Exploring the castle's battlements and towers is a must.

1.2 *Château d'Isenbourg*

Nestled between vineyards, Château d'Isenbourg emanates elegance and charm. Its sophisticated accommodations, exquisite cuisine, and spa amenities make it a wonderful option for a romantic retreat.

1.3 *Staying in a Castle:*

Experience the grandeur of the past while enjoying contemporary facilities. Many castle motels provide magnificent apartments, good cuisine, and guided excursions that give insights into the region's history.

2. Vineyard Lodgings

3.1 *Les Prés d'Ondine*

This charming guesthouse is bordered by vineyards and provides magnificent views of the Alsace countryside. Guests may enjoy wine tastings, leisurely walks, and tranquil moments in the middle of nature.

2.2 *La Maison des Chanoines*

Experience life in a small town by staying at La Maison des Chanoines. This vineyard hotel enables visitors to immerse themselves in local life while enjoying closeness to vineyards and wineries.

2.3 *Staying at a Vineyard Lodge:*

Vineyard lodgings give a unique chance to discover rural Alsace. Expect tranquil vistas, bespoke wine experiences, and an opportunity to meet with local winemakers.

3. Practical Tips

3.1 *Best Time to Visit*

Spring and autumn are perfect for beautiful weather and fewer visitors, making it easier to explore the region's various lodgings.

3.2 *Booking Your Stay*

Castle and vineyard hotels might be in great demand, so it's wise to book well in advance to ensure your favorite dates.

3.3 **Cultural Etiquette**

Familiarize yourself with local traditions and etiquette, including simple French words, to better your interactions with locals.

CHAPTER 8

PLANNING YOUR ALSACE ITINERARY

• RECOMMENDED DURATION OF STAY

1. **Exploration of Strasbourg:** Strasbourg, the capital of Alsace, is a must-visit site. Its well-preserved medieval buildings, cobblestone alleyways, and the spectacular Strasbourg Cathedral deserve at least two days of investigation. Spend time meandering around La Petite France, a historic region famed for its timber-framed buildings and lovely waterways. Explore the Grande Île, a UNESCO World Heritage site, and take a boat cruise down the Ill River to acquire a unique view of the city.

2. **Wine Route and Vineyard Visits:** Alsace is famed for its wine production, and the Alsace Wine Route is a tour through scenic vineyards, wineries, and small towns. To properly enjoy the trip, allow at least three days to explore this route. Visit vineyards in places including Riquewihr, Ribeauvillé, and Eguisheim, sampling a selection of Alsatian wines and learning about the winemaking process.

3. **Picturesque Villages and Countryside**: The region's picturesque villages are a big magnet for travelers. Consider spending an extra two to three days seeing these places at a slow pace. Each village has a different ambiance and architectural style. Obernai, Hunawihr,

and Kaysersberg are among the settlements worth investigating. Enjoy strolls, eat classic Alsatian food, and immerse yourself in the local way of life.

4. **Outdoor Activities:** For outdoor lovers, the Vosges Mountains provide a choice of activities such as hiking, bicycling, and skiing, depending on the season. If you're interested in outdoor excursions, schedule aside a minimum of two days for these activities. The magnificent vistas and pure mountain air give a pleasant contrast to the rural and city experiences.

5. **Cultural and Historical Exploration:** To dig into the historical and cultural elements of Alsace, devote an extra two days for excursions to museums, castles, and historical sites. The Haut-Koenigsbourg Castle, the Unterlinden Museum in Colmar, and the Alsatian Museum in Strasbourg give insights into the region's rich history and legacy.

6. **Culinary Delights:** Alsace is recognized for its wonderful cuisine, distinguished by robust meals and unusual tastes. Dedicate at least one day to relishing in Alsatian delicacies. Enjoy meals like choucroute garnie (sauerkraut with sausages), tarte flambée (Alsatian pizza), and local pastries. Explore local markets and cuisine festivals to experience genuine delicacies.

7. **Flexible rest:** Including a few days of rest in your schedule is vital. It enables you to absorb the ambiance, revisit your favorite sites, or just relax in the picturesque surroundings. This free time also provides for unexpected discoveries and encounters with locals that may give a personal touch to your visit.

• TIPS FOR EFFICIENT SIGHTSEEING

1. **Organize Ahead:** Before leaving on your Alsace excursion, take the time to study and organize your schedule. Identify the important attractions, historical places, and natural marvels you'd want to see. Create a flexible schedule that allows for both exploration and rest.

2. **Choose Your Base Wisely**: Select a central place as your base, such as Strasbourg or Colmar. This deliberate move will decrease travel time between sites and give the convenience of returning to a familiar spot each night.

3. **Explore the Villages:** Alsace is famed for its lovely villages with half-timbered buildings and flower-bedecked alleys. Wander around Eguisheim, Riquewihr, and Kaysersberg to explore the region's original flavor and architecture.

4. **Embrace the gastronomic Delights:** Indulge in Alsace's gastronomic wonders, such as tarte flambée (Alsatian pizza), choucroute garnie (sauerkraut with sausages), and foie gras. Pair

your meals with local wines like Riesling and Gewürztraminer to improve the dining experience.

5. **Visit the Strasbourg Cathedral:** The Strasbourg Cathedral, a marvel of Gothic architecture, is a must-see. Climb to the summit for panoramic views of the city and the surrounding countryside.

6. **Experience the Alsace Wine Route:** Embark on the famed Alsace Wine Route, which travels past vineyards and lovely towns. Stop at wineries along the trip for samples and to learn about the winemaking process.

7. **Explore the Alsace Regional Natural Park**: Nature aficionados will adore the Alsace Regional Natural Park. Hike across varied settings, including woods, marshes, and rolling hills. The park is a good area for birding and relaxing.

8. **Discover Historical Sites:** Alsace possesses a rich past, represented in its castles, fortresses, and museums. Visit Haut-Koenigsbourg Castle for a look into medieval life and the Maginot Line for insight into World War II.

9. **Time Your Visits Wisely:** To avoid crowds and get the most out of your touring, try to visit famous places early in the morning or late in the day. This strategy enables you to appreciate the attractions with fewer visitors.

10. **Learn Some Basic French words**: While many people in Alsace speak English, learning a few basic French words will enrich your contacts with locals and demonstrate your admiration for their culture.

11. **Respect Local traditions**: Take an effort to study and respect local traditions, such as shop opening hours, dining etiquette, and traditional greetings. This will help you blend in and create a great impression.

12. **Immerse Yourself in Festivals:** Alsace holds many festivals throughout the year, honoring anything from wine and flowers to music and Christmas markets. Attending these events gives unique cultural experiences and an opportunity to engage with locals.

13. **Utilize Public Transportation**: Consider utilizing the excellent public transportation system in Alsace. Trains and buses link major cities and villages, making it simple to move between sites without the stress of driving.

14. **Capture Memories:** Bring a camera or smartphone to capture the beauty of Alsace. The region's magnificent vistas and lovely towns provide superb picture opportunities.

15. **Be Open to Serendipity**: While preparation is vital, be open to surprising discoveries. Some of the most unforgettable moments

occur when you stumble onto hidden treasures and unanticipated excursions.

CHAPTER 9

PRACTICAL INFORMATION AND TRAVEL TIPS
CURRENCY

Currency

The official currency of Alsace, as well as the whole nation of France, is the Euro (€), indicated by the currency code EUR. The Euro is split into 100 smaller units called cents (¢). Banknotes and coins are regularly used for transactions, with the following denominations:

Banknotes:

€5 €10 €20 €50 €100 €200 €500 (less usually used)

Coins:

1 cent (€0.01)

2 cents (€0.02)

5 cents (€0.05)

10 cents (€0.10)

20 cents (€0.20)

50 cents (€0.50)

€1 €2

It's good to carry a mix of both banknotes and coins for your everyday spending, since some smaller places may prefer cash transactions.

Currency Exchange

Currency exchange facilities are readily accessible across Alsace, particularly in major tourist regions and at airports. Banks, currency exchange bureaus, and even some hotels provide currency exchange services. While these services are handy, it's crucial to be aware of the conversion rates and any related costs or charges, which might fluctuate.

To guarantee you achieve a good exchange rate, examine the following tips:

Compare rates from multiple exchange providers before making a purchase.

Avoid converting cash at airports, since rates tend to be less beneficial.

Inform your bank about your vacation intentions to prevent any complications with your credit/debit cards.

Payment Methods

In Alsace, like in much of Europe, electronic payment methods are extensively accepted. Major credit and debit cards such as Visa,

MasterCard, and American Express are routinely used at restaurants, stores, hotels, and other venues. Contactless payments are also widespread, particularly for minor transactions.

ATMs (Automated Teller Machines) are commonly located in cities and towns, enabling you to withdraw Euros with your debit or credit card. However, be careful of any withdrawal costs imposed by your bank and the local ATM operator.

Tipping Etiquette

Tipping procedures in Alsace are identical to the rest of France. While service costs are sometimes included in restaurant bills, it's common to offer a tiny extra tip for exceptional treatment. A normal gratuity is roughly 5-10% of the entire price. When tipping, you may either deliver the tip straight to the waitress or leave it on the table.

Budgeting and Expenses

Alsace provides a multitude of possibilities for various budgets. The cost of housing, food, and activities might vary based on the place you're visiting and the amount of luxury you choose. On average, a mid-range visitor should anticipate spending roughly €70-100 per day, including hotel, food, transportation, and some sightseeing.

• LANGUAGE ABD COMMUNICATION

1. Language in Alsace

1.1. *Official Languages*

The primary language spoken in Alsace is French. However, due to its historical ties with Germany, Alsatian (also known as Alsacien) is a regional dialect that's still spoken by some locals. Alsatian is a Germanic language, which adds to the linguistic diversity of the region.

1.2. *Basic Phrases in French*

Learning a few key phrases in French can greatly enhance your travel experience:

Bonjour: Hello

Merci: Thank you

S'il vous plaît: Please

Oui: Yes

Non: No

Parlez-vous anglais?: Do you speak English?

Excusez-moi: Excuse me

2.3. *Alsatian Phrases*

While not necessary, learning a few Alsatian phrases can be a charming way to connect with the locals:

Elsässisch ist schee!: Alsatian is beautiful!

Guten Tag: Good day (Alsatian version)

Gueter Owet: Good evening (Alsatian version)

2. Communication Tips

2.1. Language Considerations

Most locals in urban areas, especially those involved in the tourism industry, will speak English. However, in more rural areas, English proficiency might be limited. Carrying a phrasebook or a translation app can be extremely helpful.

2.2. Politeness and Etiquette

French culture places a strong emphasis on politeness and formalities. When addressing someone, especially those older than you, using titles like "Monsieur" (Mr.) or "Madame" (Mrs.) is appreciated.

2.3. Non-Verbal Communication

Non-verbal cues, such as handshakes and maintaining eye contact, are important in Alsace. A firm handshake is a common greeting, and maintaining eye contact shows respect and engagement in conversations.

3. Cultural Insights

3.1. *Gastronomy and Communication*

Alsace is renowned for its exquisite cuisine, including sauerkraut, flammekueche, and the famous Alsace wines. When dining, engaging in discussions about food and wine is a fantastic way to connect with locals. Complementing the chef with "C'était délicieux!" (It was delicious!) is a gesture that will be appreciated.

3.2. *Festivals and Celebrations*

Participating in local festivals, such as the Strasbourg Christmas Market, is a great way to immerse yourself in the culture. Engaging in conversations during these events will provide insights into traditional customs and practices.

4. Navigating Alsace

4.1. *Transportation and Communication*

Public transportation, including trains and buses, is efficient and widely used. While signage is usually in both French and English, having a basic understanding of French can help you navigate more smoothly.

4.2. *Asking for Directions*

If you need directions, approach locals politely and start the conversation with a friendly "Excusez-moi, pourriez-vous m'aider?" (Excuse me, could you help me?). Most people will be happy to assist.

5. **Language Learning Resources**

If you're interested in delving deeper into the local language, consider using language learning apps like Duolingo or taking online courses. This will not only enrich your travel experience but also allow you to connect more authentically with the local community.

• SAFETY AND EMERGENCY CONTACTS

1. General Safety Tips

a. *Health Precautions*

Health Insurance: Make sure you have adequate travel health insurance that covers medical emergencies, hospitalization, and repatriation.

Drugs: Carry an extra supply of any prescription drugs you need, along with a copy of your prescription. Research nearby pharmacies for refills if required.

Medical Allergies: If you have allergies or certain medical problems, consider wearing a medical alert bracelet and bring the required medical paperwork.

b. *Personal Safety*

Stay Informed: Familiarize yourself with the local culture, regulations, and possible hazards in Alsace. Stay updated about current events and any travel warnings issued by your government.

Secure Belongings: Avoid exhibiting precious objects like jewelry and gadgets. Use hotel safes for passports, extra cash, and other valuables.

Public transit: Be mindful of your surroundings when utilizing public transit. Keep a watch on your valuables and be careful of your stops.

Strolling at Night: Stick to well-lit areas while strolling at night and avoid poorly lit or lonely streets.

2. Emergency Contacts

a. *Police and Emergency Services*

Police: 17

Contact the police in case of non-urgent circumstances or to report minor incidents.

Medical Emergencies: 15

Dial this number for emergency medical help or an ambulance.

Fire Department: 18

In case of fires or other emergencies, call the fire department.

b. *Embassy and Consulate*

It's important to have your embassy or consulate's contact information in case you suffer legal troubles, lose your passport, or seek help from your home country.

c. *Local Hospitals*

Research and take down the contact information of hospitals or medical facilities near your accommodation or trip locations.

3. Natural Hazards and Weather

Alsace enjoys diverse weather conditions throughout the year. Check weather predictions before going and be prepared for changes.

a. *Flooding*

Some places in Alsace are prone to flooding, especially following heavy rainfall. Stay updated about weather warnings and avoid flood-prone zones.

c. *Winter Conditions*

During the winter months, snow and ice may make roads and sidewalks treacherous. Drive safely and equip your vehicle with adequate tires if required.

4. *Cultural Sensitivity*

Respect the local culture and traditions to create a peaceful experience:

Language: While many people speak English, mastering a few basic French words may go a long way in communicating.

Dress Code: When visiting religious places or rural regions, dress modestly and respectfully.

• LOCAL CUSTOMS AND ETIQUETTE

1. Greetings and Politeness

Alsace has a warm and welcoming culture and welcomes play a vital part in everyday encounters. When greeting someone, a simple "Bonjour" (hello) or "Bonsoir" (good evening) accompanied by a grin is common. Handshakes are popular in official contexts, but among friends and acquaintances, a gentle kiss on both cheeks is a normal method to welcome. When leaving, it's acceptable to say "Au revoir" (goodbye) with a grin.

2. Language

French is the major language spoken in Alsace, although owing to the region's closeness to Germany, many inhabitants are also competent in German.

It's a good idea to learn a few simple words in both languages to demonstrate your appreciation for the local culture. While English is widely spoken in tourist regions, attempting to converse in French or German is welcomed and may help you connect with the people.

3. Dining Etiquette

Dining is a treasured social activity in Alsace, and there are particular etiquette guidelines to bear in mind:

Table Manners: Keep your hands on the table at all times; resting your wrists on the edge of the table is considered disrespectful. Remember to keep your elbows off the table as well.

Bread Etiquette: Place your bread on the table, not on your plate. Break off little pieces and butter them separately, rather than buttering the whole slice at once.

Wine Toasts: When clinking glasses for a toast, keep eye contact with the person you're toasting. Additionally, it's customary to yell "Santé!" while gazing directly into the person's eyes. (cheers) or "Prost!" (German for cheers).

Tipping: Service costs are frequently included in restaurant bills, however leaving a little tip is appreciated. Rounding up the amount or leaving a few extra euros is a regular habit.

4. Dress Code

Alsace is famed for its attractive villages and sophisticated towns, so wearing properly and slightly formally is a gesture of respect. While casual wear is suitable for daily touring, consider dressing up somewhat for evenings at excellent restaurants or for attending cultural activities.

5. Public Behavior Queueing

Alsace has a long history of orderly queueing. Always wait your turn in line, whether it's at a bus stop, at a shop, or a ticket desk.

Public settings: Keep your voice down in public settings, such as public transit and museums. Loud chats could be deemed disruptive.

Smoking: Smoking is forbidden in most indoor public locations, including restaurants and public transit. Look for approved smoking spaces if you need to smoke.

6. Gift Giving

If you're invited to someone's house, bringing a modest gift is a considerate gesture. Flowers, a bottle of wine, or a box of chocolates are common alternatives. When offering a gift, give it with both hands as a display of respect.

7. Cultural Sensitivity

War History: Alsace has a complicated history including battles between France and Germany. While discussing war-related themes, be attentive to the historical context and the emotions that may be associated with these matters.

Religion: Alsace has a variety of religious views, principally Catholicism and Protestantism. Be respectful of religious places, traditions, and customs, even if you don't share the same views.

• PACKING ESSENTIALS

1. Clothing:

Weather-Appropriate Attire: Alsace encounters a variety of weather conditions. Pack lightweight, breathable garments for the summer months, like short-sleeve shirts, shorts, and sundresses. However, Alsace winters may be chilly, so carry warm layers, including sweaters, coats, and thermal underwear.

Comfortable Walking Shoes: You'll likely spend a lot of time touring Alsace on foot. Pack comfy walking shoes that give support and cushioning.

Rain Gear: Alsace is renowned for its occasional showers. Don't forget to carry a tiny umbrella or a waterproof jacket to remain dry.

2. Travel Documents:

Passport and ID: Ensure your passport is valid for at least six months beyond your trip dates. Carry a photocopy of your passport and a government-issued ID as a backup.

Visa Requirements: Check whether you need a visa to enter France and ensure you have the relevant documentation.

Travel Insurance: Accidents and unforeseen incidents might happen. Travel insurance gives a piece of mind in case of medical crises, travel cancellations, or misplaced baggage.

Paper Itinerary: While digital versions are helpful, having a paper copy of your itinerary, lodging information, and key contact numbers may be a lifesaver if your gadgets run out of charge.

3. Electronics:

Universal Power Adapter: Alsace utilizes the European standard Type C and Type E power outlets. A universal adaptor will guarantee your gadgets remain charged.

Cell Phone and Charger: Stay connected with your loved ones and traverse the area with your cell phone. Make sure you enable international roaming or buy a local SIM card.

Camera and Accessories: Capture the beauty of Alsace with a camera, additional batteries, memory cards, and any required lenses.

4. Toiletries and Medications:

Amenities Kit: Pack travel-sized amenities, including shampoo, conditioner, soap, toothpaste, and a toothbrush.

Prescription drugs: Bring enough of your prescription drugs to last the length of your vacation. Carry a copy of your medicines and a doctor's letter for customs if required.

First Aid Kit: A simple first aid kit containing adhesive bandages, painkillers, disinfectant wipes, and any personal prescriptions may be quite handy.

5. **Money and Payment:**

Currency: The currency used in Alsace is the Euro (€). Carry some local cash for modest purchases, but depend on credit/debit cards for most transactions.

Credit/Debit Cards: Notify your bank about your trip dates to prevent any complications with using your cards overseas. Credit cards are commonly accepted, but having extra cash on hand is usually a smart idea.

6. **Miscellaneous:**

Language Guide: While many people in Alsace understand English, possessing a basic French phrasebook or language app will boost your interactions with locals.

Reusable Water Bottle: Stay hydrated while reducing your environmental effect by carrying a reusable water bottle.

Daypack or Backpack: A compact backpack for day travel would be great to carry your things while traveling.

Snacks: Pack some energy bars or snacks for lengthy flights or times when you may not find a good dinner choice.

- ## ANNUAL FESTIVALS AND CELEBRATIONS

1. Carnival of Mulhouse

Date: February - March

Dive into the joyful atmosphere with the Carnival of Mulhouse, a boisterous and colorful event that commemorates the end of winter. Marvel at magnificent parades including carefully crafted floats, bright costumes, and traditional music. Join residents and tourists in the streets as they dance, sing, and enjoy delectable Alsatian sweets. The carnival gives a wonderful peek into the local culture and its links to past rituals.

2. Alsace Wine Route Festival

Date: August

Wine connoisseurs delight during the Alsace Wine Route Festival, a celebration of the region's world-renowned wines. Explore the picturesque towns along the famed Alsace Wine Route, where local winemakers offer their cellars for tastings and tours. Engage in wine-related activities, enjoy live music, and experience amazing food pairings that complement the superb wines produced in this scenic area.

3. Strasbourg Christmas Market

Date: Late November - December

Immerse yourself in the magnificent aura of the Strasbourg Christmas Market, one of the oldest and most charming holiday marketplaces in Europe. Wander through festively adorned kiosks selling homemade decorations, warm mulled wine, and regional delights like gingerbread and roasted chestnuts. The beautiful background of Strasbourg's historic buildings surrounded by shimmering lights offers an amazing winter paradise.

4. Colmar Jazz Festival

Date: September

Music fans are in for a treat at the Colmar Jazz Festival, an annual event that turns the streets and venues of Colmar into a musical refuge. Experience a broad variety of jazz performers, spanning from classic to current forms.

The festival's unique combination of world-class artists, historic venues, and the town's beautiful aura makes it a must-visit for both jazz enthusiasts and casual listeners.

5. Hopla Festival in Strasbourg

Date: July

Celebrate the Alsatian way of life at the Hopla Festival in Strasbourg. This vibrant celebration promotes the region's traditions via dancing, music, and gastronomic pleasures. Enjoy typical Alsatian foods such as sauerkraut, flammekueche, and tarte aux quetsches. The festival's emphasis on conserving local tradition and promoting a feeling of community makes it a wonderful experience for guests of all ages.

6. Fête de la Musique

Date: June 21

Join the worldwide festival of music on the streets of Alsace during the Fête de la Musique. This festival honors the summer solstice and encourages artists of various genres to play in open-air locations. Wander around the lovely squares and alleyways of Alsace's villages and cities, where you'll witness spontaneous performances that generate an atmosphere of solidarity and creativity.

7. Easter Markets in Strasbourg

Date: March - April

Experience the joyous mood of Easter in Alsace via the lovely Easter Markets of Strasbourg. Delight in finely created Easter décor, hand-painted eggs, and handcrafted products. Indulge in the local gastronomic delicacies connected with the event, such as lamb dishes and Easter desserts. The markets are a fantastic chance to explore the region's precise workmanship and welcoming friendliness.

CONCLUSION

In conclusion, the ALSACE Travel Guide for 2023-2024 provides a comprehensive and informative resource for tourists eager to discover the enchanting area of Alsace. This book gives a full and up-to-date account of the region's rich cultural past, breathtaking landscapes, and distinctive combination of French and German influences. From gorgeous towns decorated with half-timbered homes to world-renowned vineyards producing great wines, the tour illustrates the vast variety of experiences Alsace has to offer.

Travelers may discover vital information about historical monuments, local food, outdoor activities, and colorful festivals that exhibit the region's traditions and way of life. The guide's carefully chosen suggestions guarantee that tourists can make the most of their stay in Alsace, whether they are interested in walking through quaint cobblestone alleys, indulging in delicious food, or immersing themselves in the region's intriguing history.

The ALSACE Travel Guide not only acts as a useful travel companion but also kindles a feeling of anticipation and enthusiasm for the trip ahead. By giving insights into hidden treasures, transit alternatives, and hotel ideas, the book encourages tourists to design bespoke itineraries that correspond with their interests and preferences.

As a tribute to the guide's thoroughness, it not only covers renowned tourist spots but also promotes exploration of lesser-known parts of Alsace, enabling tourists to unearth the real character of the region. By encouraging ethical and courteous travel, the guide helps to the preservation of Alsace's natural beauty and cultural uniqueness for future generations.

In essence, the ALSACE Travel Guide for 2023-2024 serves as an invaluable tool for anybody going on a vacation to Alsace. Its abundance of knowledge, intelligent advice, and interesting descriptions make it an invaluable companion, ensuring that tourists can thoroughly immerse themselves in the wonderful tapestry of this enthralling area.

Whether tourists are seeking architectural wonders, gastronomic pleasures, or just the fun of experiencing a new culture, this book offers them the information and inspiration to create memorable moments in the heart of Alsace.

Made in the USA
Coppell, TX
13 October 2023

22773946R00077